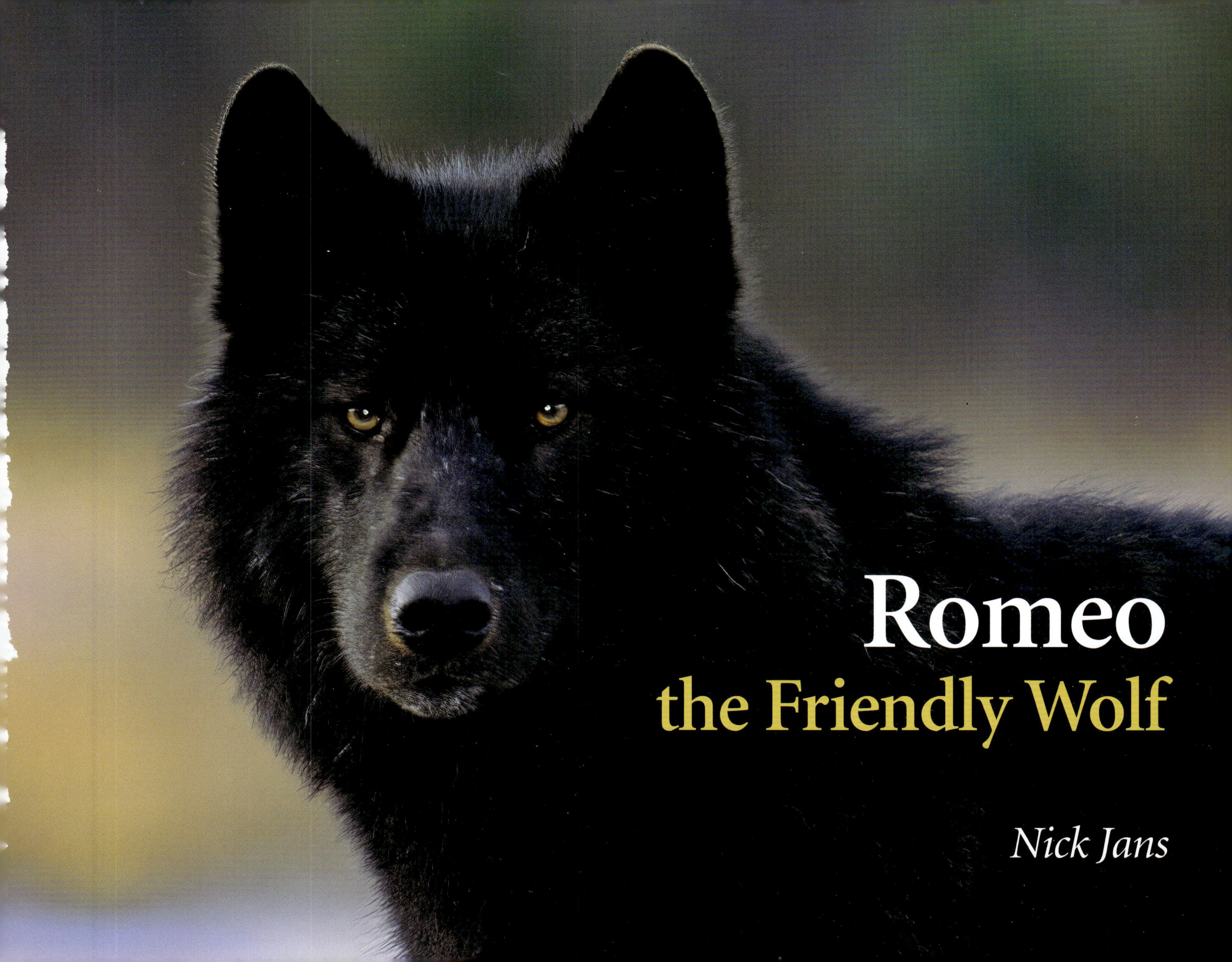

Romeo
the Friendly Wolf

Nick Jans

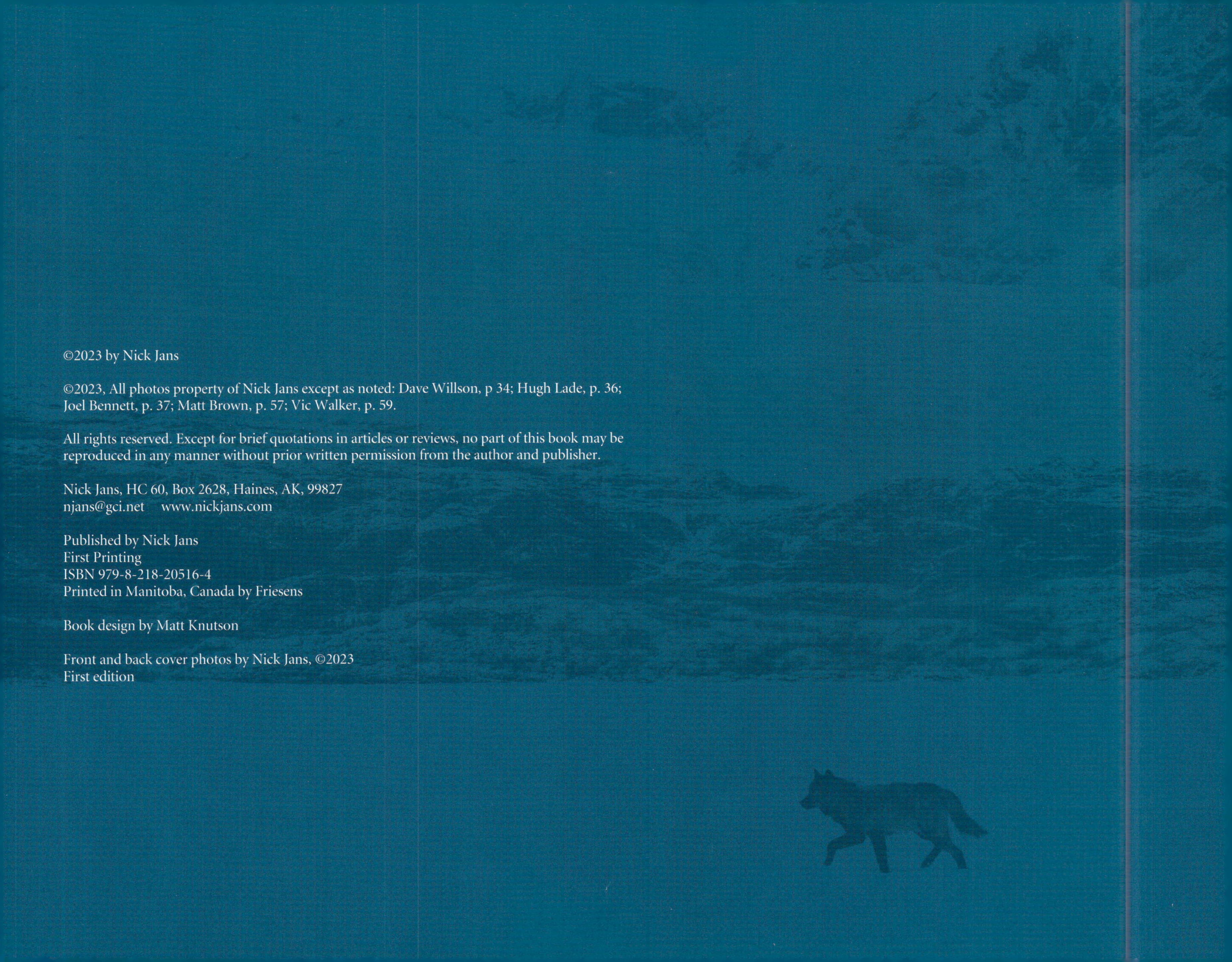

Nick Jans, HC 60, Box 2628, Haines, AK, 99827
njans@gci.net www.nickjans.com

Published by Nick Jans
First Printing
ISBN 979-8-218-20516-4
Printed in Manitoba, Canada by Friesens

Book design by Matt Knutson

Front and back cover photos by Nick Jans, ©2023
First edition

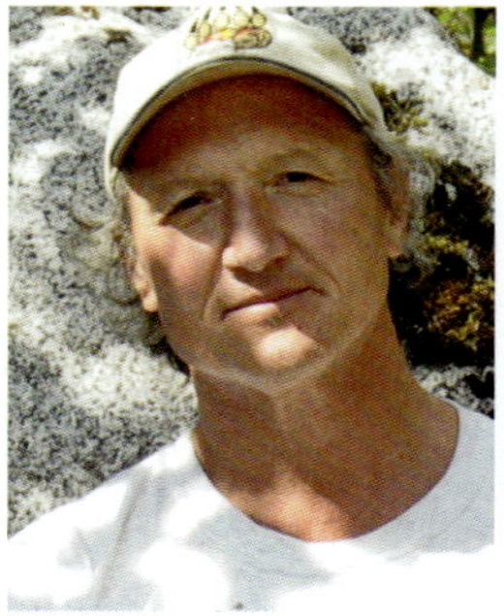

Nick Jans is one of Alaska's most recognized and prolific writers. A contributing editor to Alaska Magazine for more than three decades, he's written fourteen books and added to many others. He's also published hundreds of magazine articles and photos. Nick has been the recipient of numerous writing awards, most recently a 2022 Living Now gold medal for his national bestseller, *A Wolf Called Romeo.* He lived for 20 years in remote arctic Alaska and 20 more in the rain forests of Southeast. In recent years he's taken to wintering with his wife, Sherrie, and their dogs in the semi-boonies along north Florida's Suwannee River. He heads north as the snow melts and spends summers hanging out with grizzlies, hummingbirds, and red squirrels out the Haines Highway in between working as an Alaska storyteller on Princess Cruises. Each autumn he returns to the arctic Inupiaq village of Ambler and the surrounding country he calls home.

Books By Nick Jans

The Last Light Breaking (1993)
A Place Beyond (1996)
Tracks of the Unseen (2000)
Alaska (with photographer Art Wolfe) (2000)
The Grizzly Maze: Timothy Treadwell's Fatal Obsession With Alaskan Bears (2005)
Tracy Arm (with photographer Mark Kelley) (2006)
Alaska: A Photographic Excursion (with photographer Mark Kelley) (2007)
Black Bears of the Mendenhall Glacier (with photographer Mark Kelley) (2008)
The Glacier Wolf (2009)
Once Upon Alaska (with photographer Mark Kelley) (2013)
A Wolf Called Romeo (2014)
The Giant's Hand (2016)
Alaska's Mendenhall Glacier (with photographer Mark Kelley) (2017)

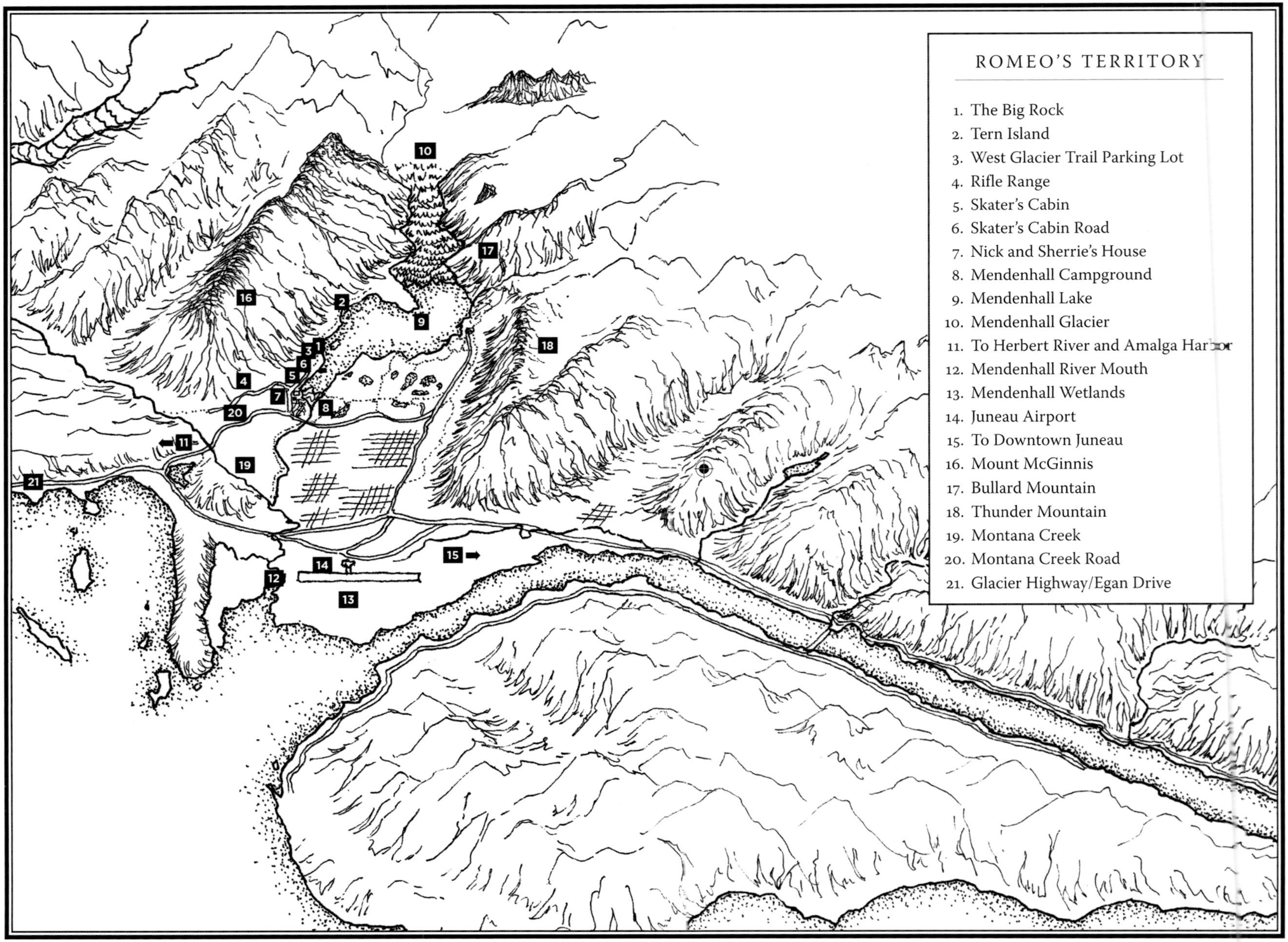
ROMEO'S TERRITORY
1. The Big Rock
2. Tern Island
3. West Glacier Trail Parking Lot
4. Rifle Range
5. Skater's Cabin
6. Skater's Cabin Road
7. Nick and Sherrie's House
8. Mendenhall Campground
9. Mendenhall Lake
10. Mendenhall Glacier
11. To Herbert River and Amalga Harbor
12. Mendenhall River Mouth
13. Mendenhall Wetlands
14. Juneau Airport
15. To Downtown Juneau
16. Mount McGinnis
17. Bullard Mountain
18. Thunder Mountain
19. Montana Creek
20. Montana Creek Road
21. Glacier Highway/Egan Drive

In memory of Vic Van Ballenberge—a man who knew wolves.
And to Romeo—A wolf who knew us.

Author's Note

More than a decade ago, I completed *A Wolf Called Romeo,* the saga of the exceptional black wolf who socialized with dogs and people in Juneau, Alaska from 2003-2009. As years have passed, his story trots onward. This telling, through words and color images combined, reflects an attempt to capture this profound experience in all its dreamlike, lucid flow and to add perspective that can only come with time. All but a few of the images are mine, taken with a variety of camera gear, most of which would be considered quaint by today's standards: a mix of slide film and early digital. All bear witness to the story as we lived it.

Acknowledgments

Creating a book is never a solitary experience. As always, I owe thanks to many: to my wife, Sherrie, for her unerring judgment and love of all living things; to Matt Knutson for his impeccable design work; to Corry Donner and Stephanie Bowens for editorial support; to Laurie Craig for her gorgeous hand-drawn map; to Vic Walker, Joel Bennet, Hugh Lade, Matt Brown, and the late David Willson for the use of images they made (see page two for page credits); and to Friesens Press for their fine printing and friendly professionalism. My deepest gratitude to the people and dogs of Juneau who witnessed and carry Romeo's story. His wild spirit lives on in our hearts.

Romeo

It's been twenty years since I first glimpsed him, and fourteen since we saw him last: a wild black wolf, washed up like a castaway on our strange shore. Scarcely a day passes that he doesn't cross my mind. His eyes follow me from wall-hung portraits and images on my laptop; a cast of his pawprint rests on a counter where I often brush my hand across it as I pass. He might as well have been a unicorn. Those tangible objects remind me that I did more than dream—I *did* know a wild wolf over six years, as he knew me and others, canine and human. We were all neighbors, that much is certain; and though some will scoff, I say friends as well. The images and words that follow are less artistic expression than attempts to explain the mystery and magic of that time—to others of course, but most importantly, to myself.

—Nick Jans, February 2023

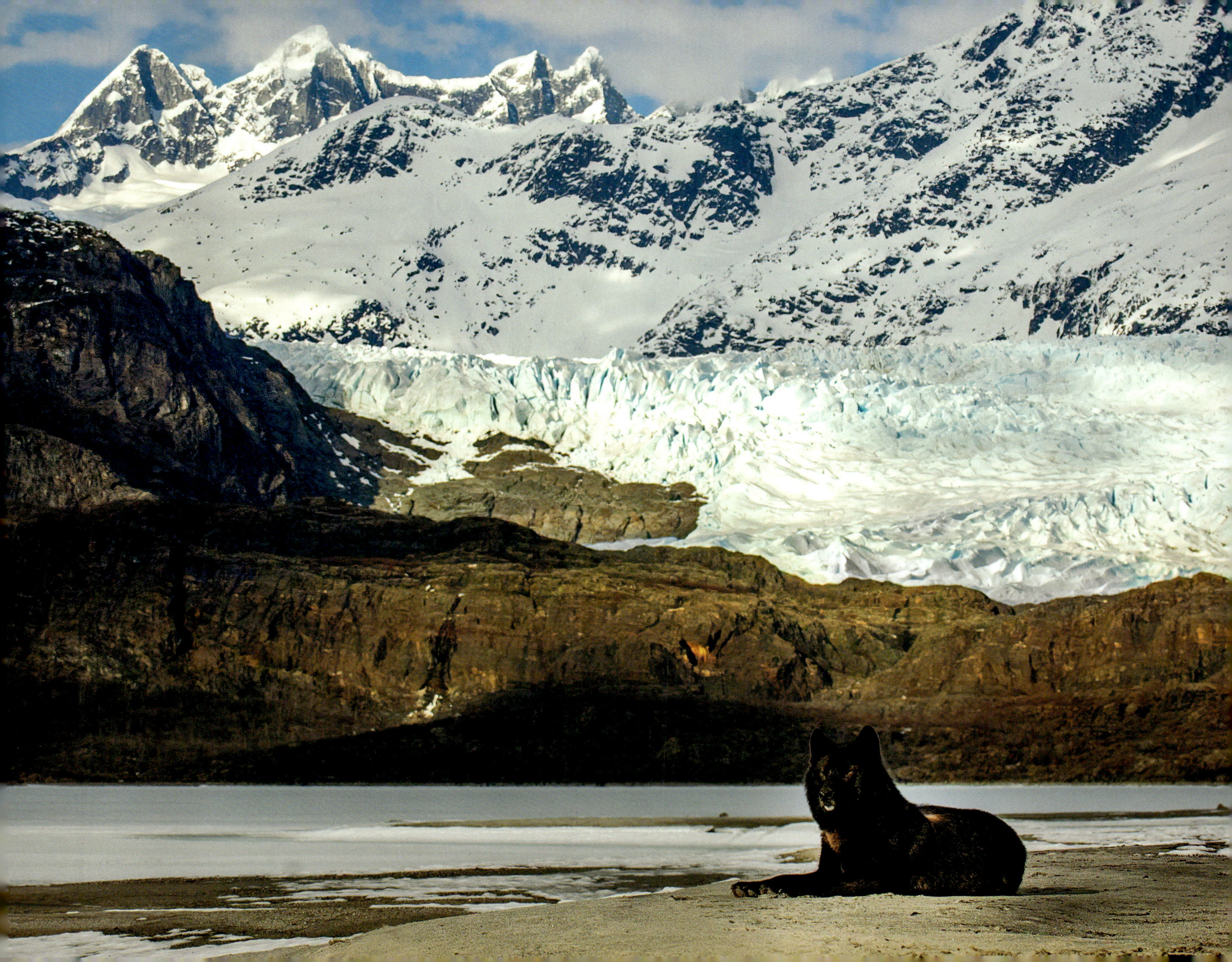

There they were: Fresh wolf tracks, broad as my palm, leading across the frozen expanse of Mendenhall Lake.

Etched in fresh snow, they passed just a few hundred yards from our house on the outskirts of Juneau, Alaska, two miles from the face of the Mendenhall Glacier. A lone traveler passing through, and small chance of glimpsing their maker, I thought. But over the next weeks more tracks appeared; and one day, at the end of them stood a wolf. Not just any wolf—a huge black male gazing toward me and my three dogs, a quarter mile away across the ice. I'd met my share of wolves over years far north, most sightings brief and hard-won. This rangy, big-framed male, though, seemed different as he stood relaxed, tail out.

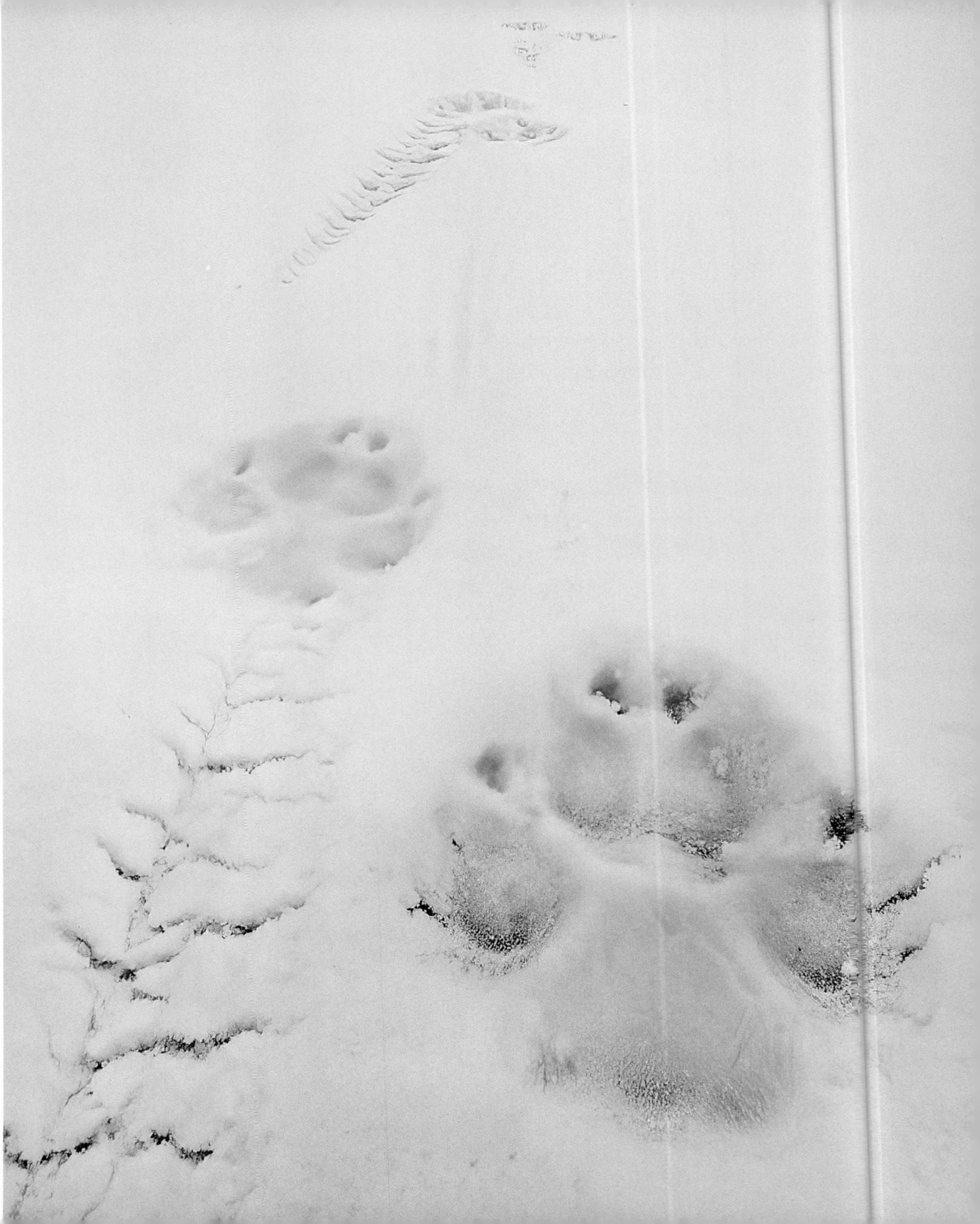

We all should have been afraid—he of me; I and my companions, of him.

After all, I, like most people, had been raised on tales—Little Red Riding Hood, Peter and the Wolf, The Three Little Pigs, and more—that whispered the same terror-edged words: *They eat us.* Likewise, any wolf that hasn't learned to run from our kind isn't long for this world.

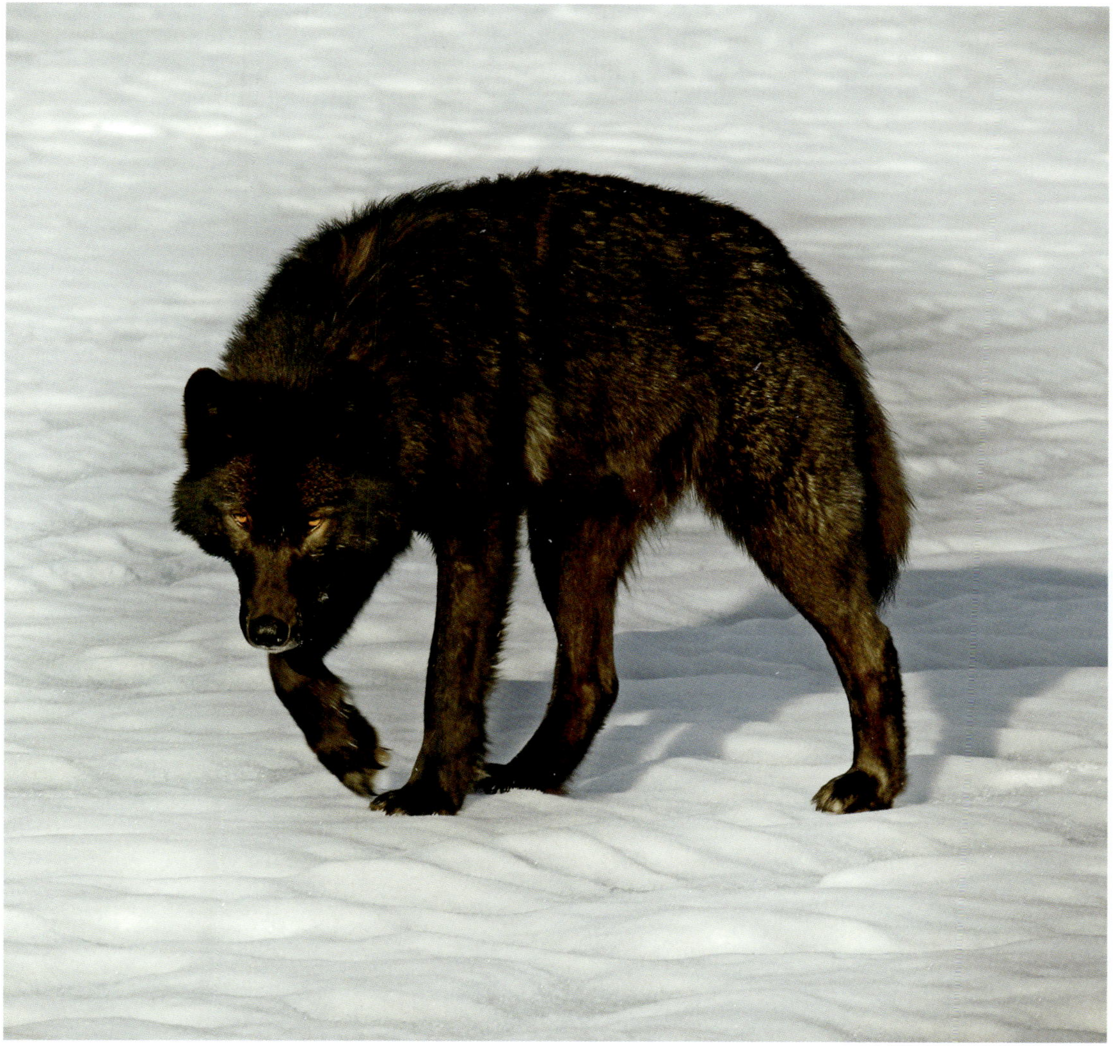

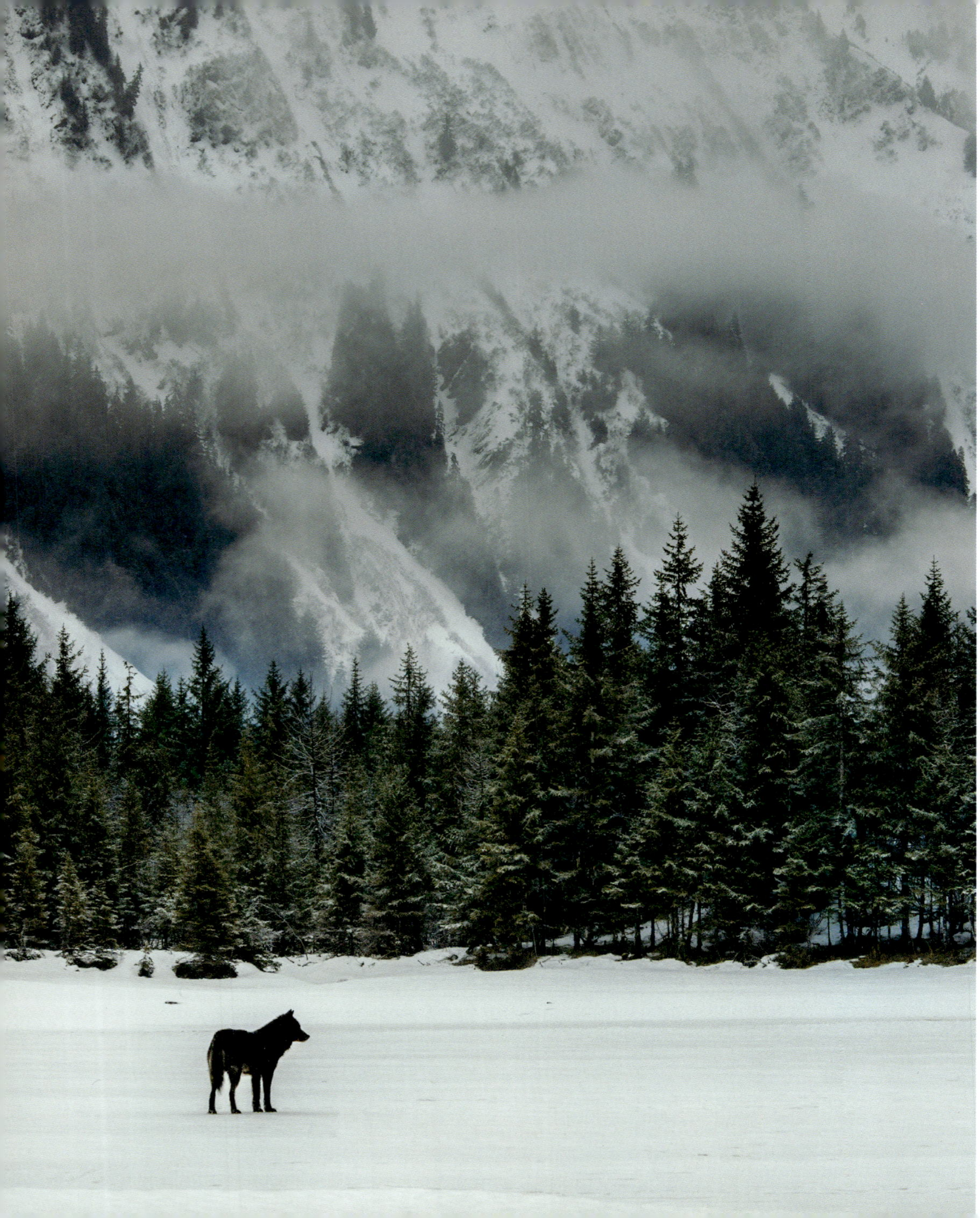

A wolf: thrilling, but not that huge a deal, right? This is Alaska, after all.

Wildlife, including grizzlies and moose, wanders close to human habitation statewide. But *canis lupus*—commonly known as the gray wolf though appearing in a variety of coloration from white to black—is spread thin across the Great Land; according to state biologists, somewhere between seven to twelve thousand wolves over more than a half million square miles. They tend to remain unseen, slipping through the spaces we leave vacant; so elusive, in fact, that most Alaskans have never heard a howl nor glimpsed a fresh track, let alone its maker. Most who have been lucky enough to spy a wolf would describe a distant speck or flash of vanishing fur.

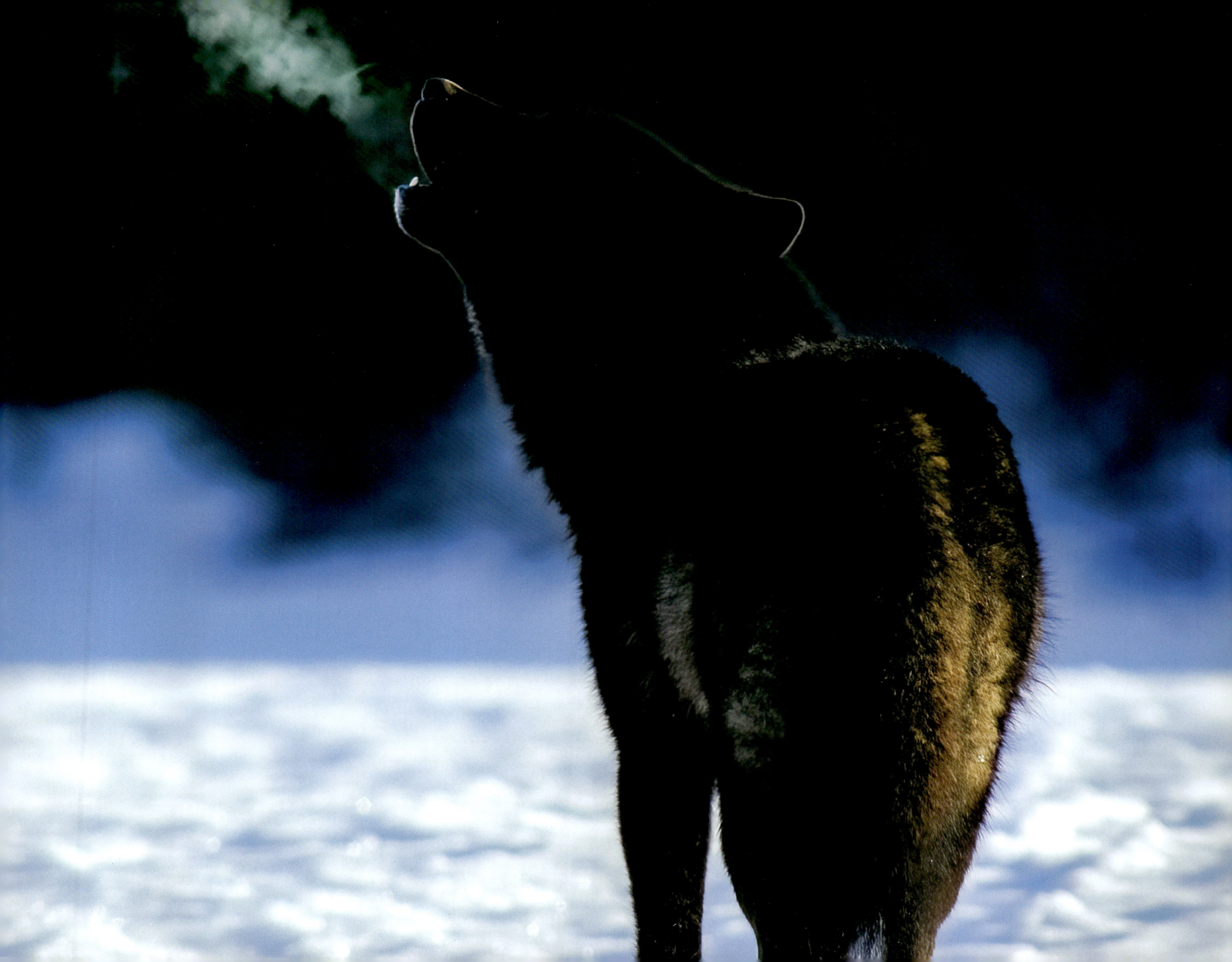

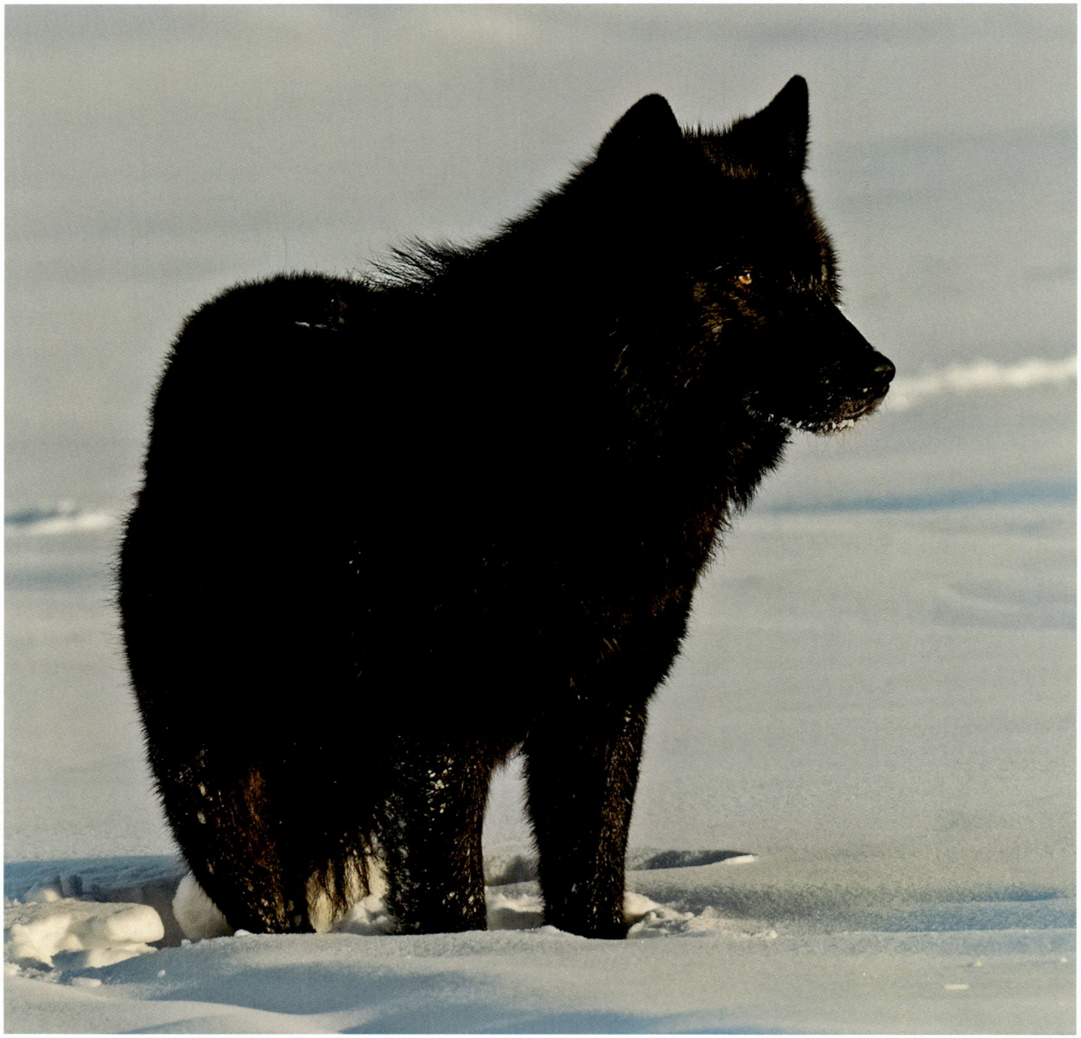

And with good reason.

Though the days of bounty hunting and poisoned bait are past, state-run predator control programs and permissive hunting and trapping regulations continue. The uncounted thousands of dead wolves not only in Alaska but worldwide over centuries are mute testament to the intertwined, conflicted relationship between the planet's two most widespread and successful large predatory mammals.

But this wolf didn't fade into the surrounding mountain-rimmed, glacier-strewn wilds as I'd expected, away from our angular, harsh-scented world. Instead, he watched from the lake edge, ghosting in and out of sight, seeming to study us as we studied him. Over the following days, I skied out and found him several times more, both alone and with one or all three of our dogs kept close. The distance began to narrow, the wolf sometimes angling toward us, or circling behind to nose our tracks; and I meandering closer, eyes averted, pausing often. But a wary space remained, as well it should.

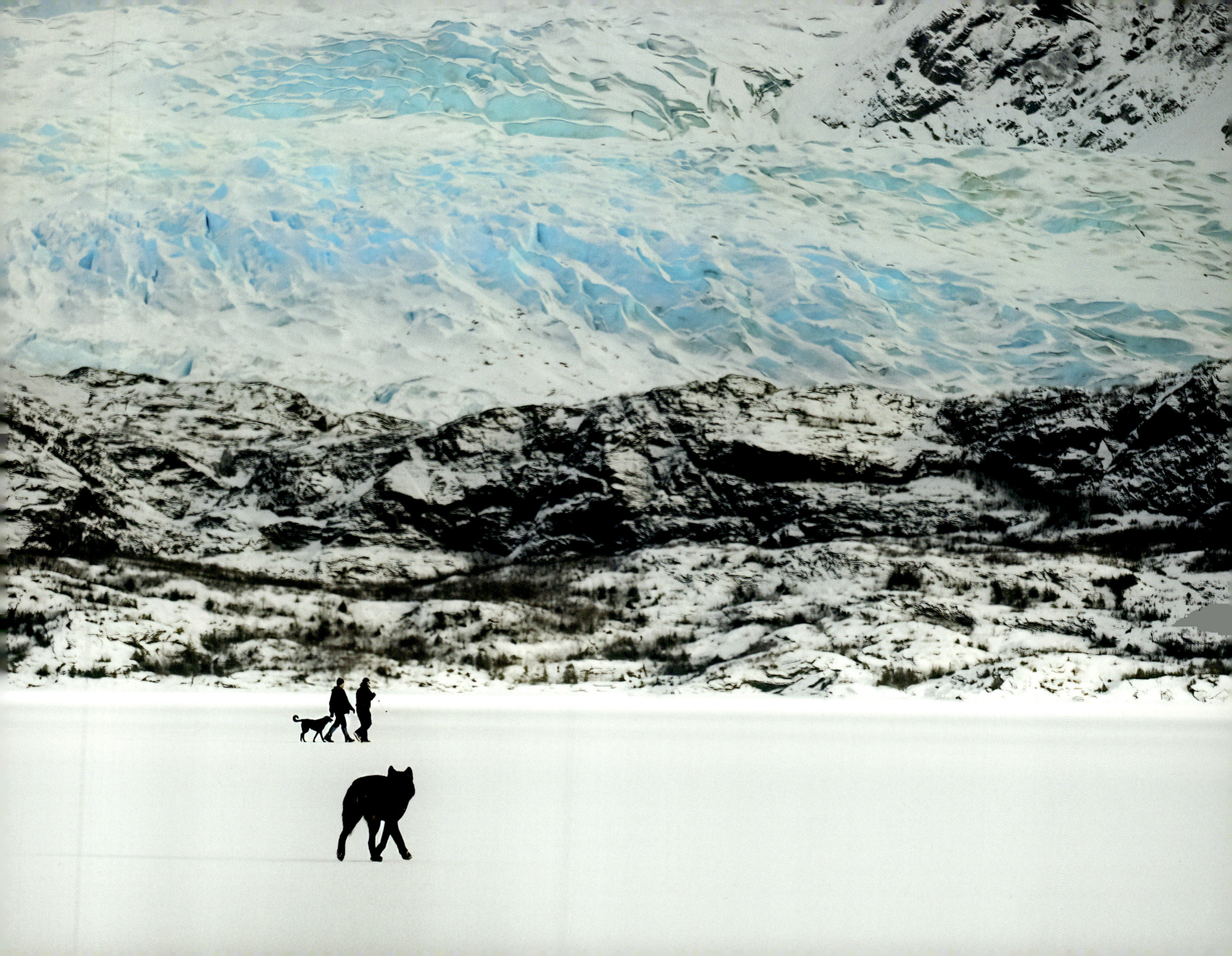

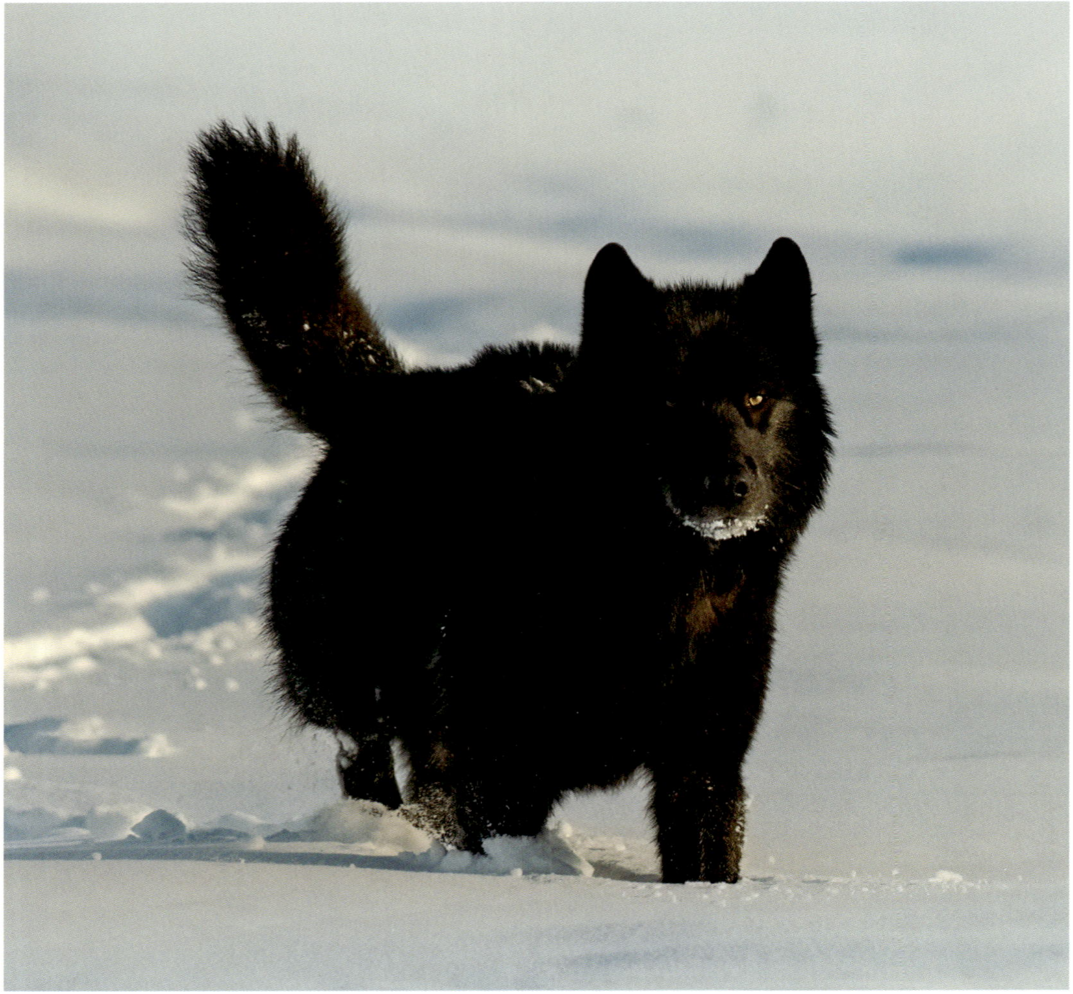

That distance evaporated in the deepening twilight of a December evening.

I'd walked out on the ice with Sherrie and our cream-colored Labrador, Dakotah, hoping to spot the wolf she'd heard about for days but not yet seen. And there he was, a shadow among shadows near the Big Rock along the shore near the West Glacier trailhead. Instead of watching from a distance, the wolf broke into a lope straight for us. Dakotah, normally well-mannered, wrenched free of my grip and ran to meet him, Sherrie's desperate calls trailing behind. They skidded to a stop and stood facing each other, muzzles a foot apart, eyes locked; the wolf's tail raised, tip gently waving, Dakotah's straight out. As the black wolf towered over her, I lifted my camera and snapped a single frame, then another. At last Dakotah returned from whatever call of the wild she'd just heard. We stood watching and wondering in the fading light as the wolf whined, a high-pitched keening that filled the silence. As the first stars flickered against the curve of space, we walked homeward, the wolf standing alone in the gathering night, his deep howls echoing off the glacier.

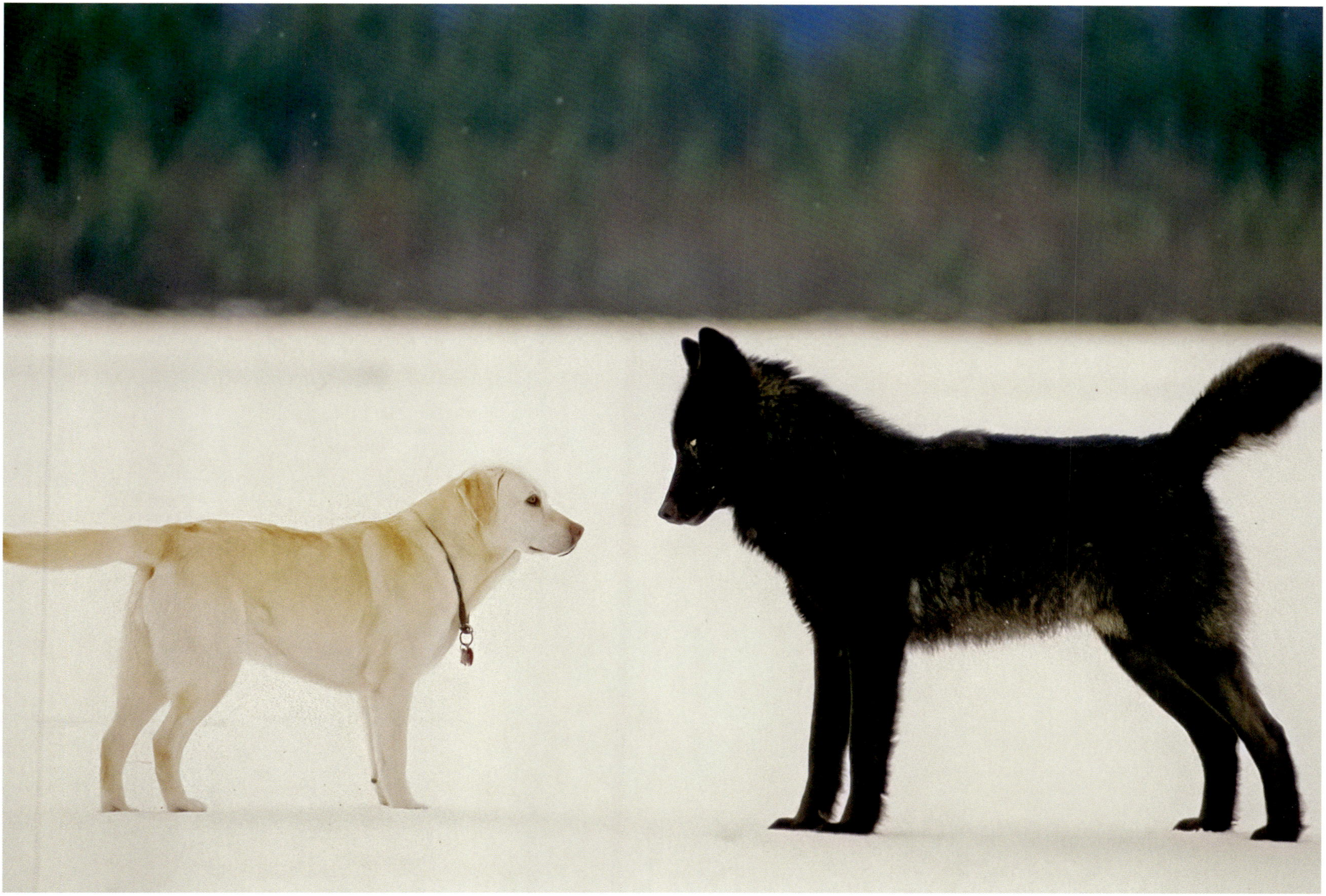

Dakotah and Romeo

From that moment, things could never be the same.

Over the following days, the wolf and I met several more times. I didn't want him too close and neither did we want to crowd him; but also didn't want to miss the opportunity just to *see* this wolf. Sherrie and I met others who'd had their own encounters. But as with us, not the least hint of aggression; and the same sort of social overtures to their dogs. One woman skier told me in a casual tone that her husky mix and the wolf had been meeting for early morning play sessions. A trio of dog walkers I met were rattled by the wolf's sudden approach to within a few paces and retreated toward the parking lot, yelling and waving, the wolf a few paces behind. Most experiences lay far inside these extremes. Some mistook the wolf for a big loose dog—though for those who knew wolves, no mistaking that straight-backed, flowing stride, that laser-like gaze.

People tended to keep those early encounters to themselves. The early winter of 2003 was marked by alternating waves of deep cold and storm. Amid the weather, brief daylight and the flurry of the holidays, visitors to the glacier were few. The presence of the black wolf remained little more than news between neighbors and friends.

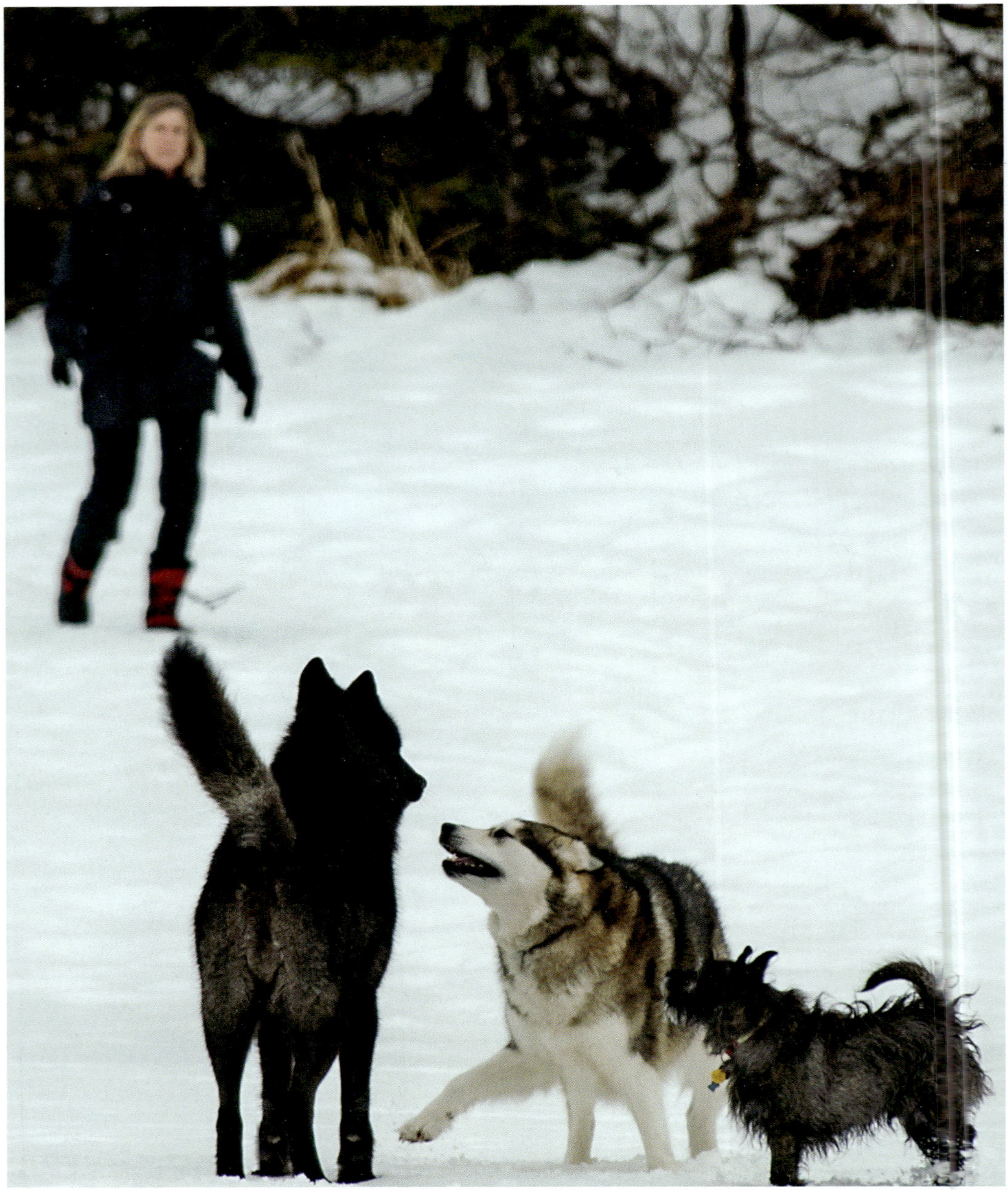

A Romeo Memory

New Kid in Town

This image was my first up-close portrait of Romeo, just a few hundred yards from our back door. I was walking the dogs when the wolf suddenly appeared from the brush. Even zoomed out with my 80-200 lens, I couldn't focus at first, which means he was closer than eight feet. This shot captures the youthful exuberance of the wolf we first met.

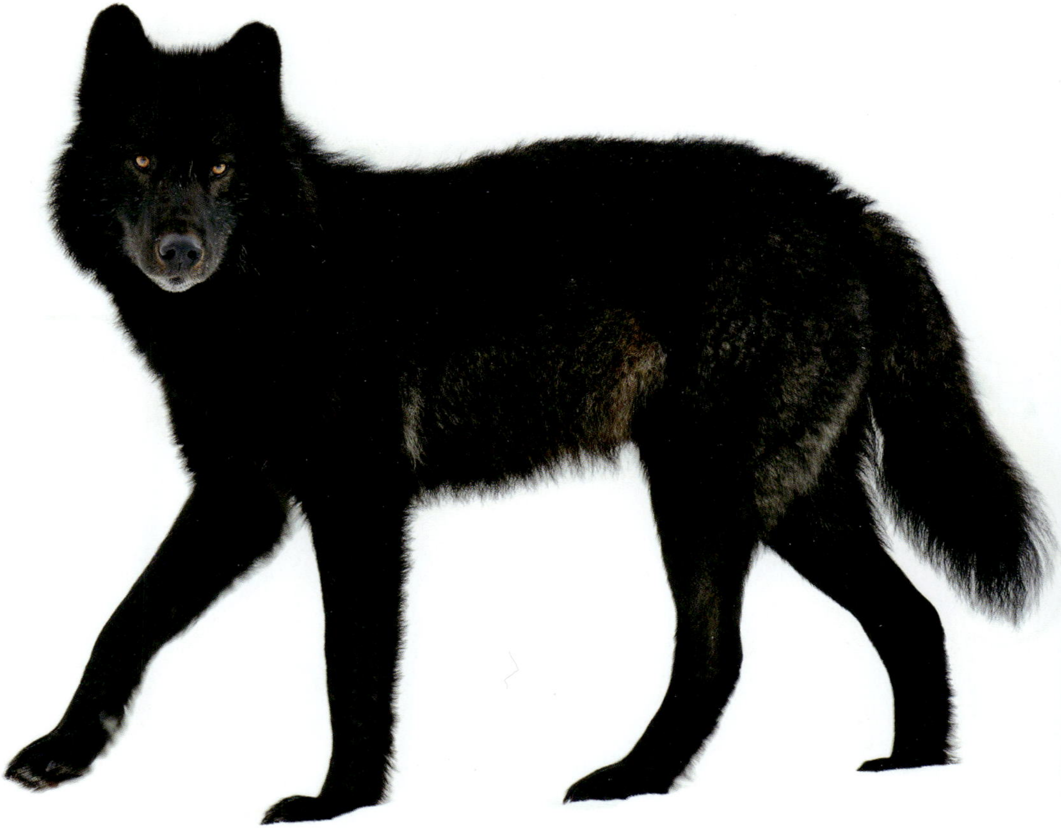

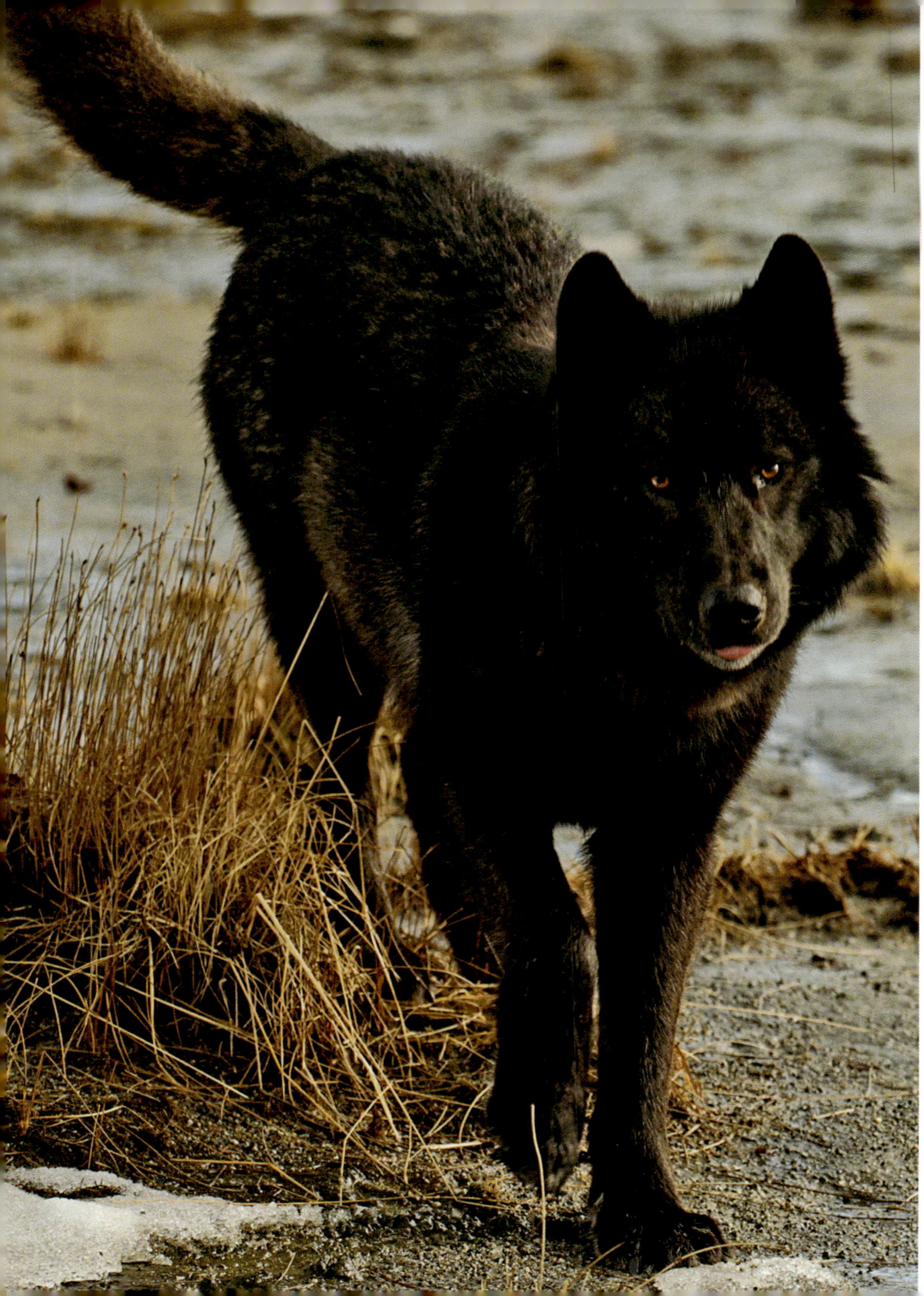

Who was this dark, handsome stranger? Where had he come from and why was he here?

Wolves live in tight-knit family groups we call packs, on the constant move within a territory often spanning hundreds of square miles. Yet this solitary animal kept appearing near the glacier and down the wooded, riverine corridor of the Mendenhall valley, drifting on the edge of neighborhoods—especially ours, the last before the glacier. I kept expecting him to vanish as suddenly as he'd appeared; a wolf's life is an endless journey, and totally unusual, aside from denning to have pups in the spring, for one to linger more than a few days in a small area, let alone so close to so many of our kind.

Though mostly black, the coloration of Romeo's coat varied with the light, his shedding cycle, and his age. He was darkest in early winter and sun-bleached by late-spring. Sunlight brought out rich, reddish-brown tints; and of course, he grizzled as the years passed.

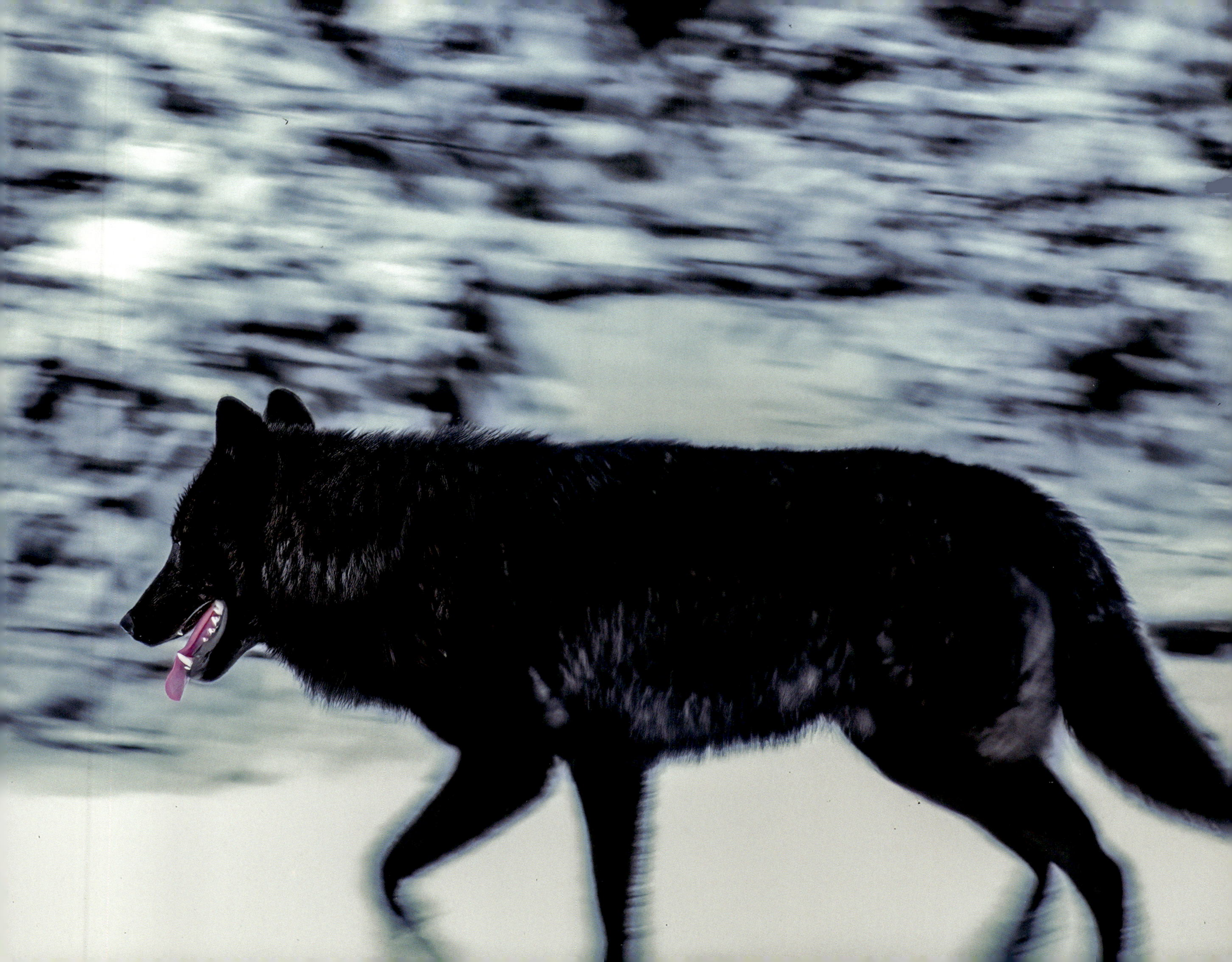

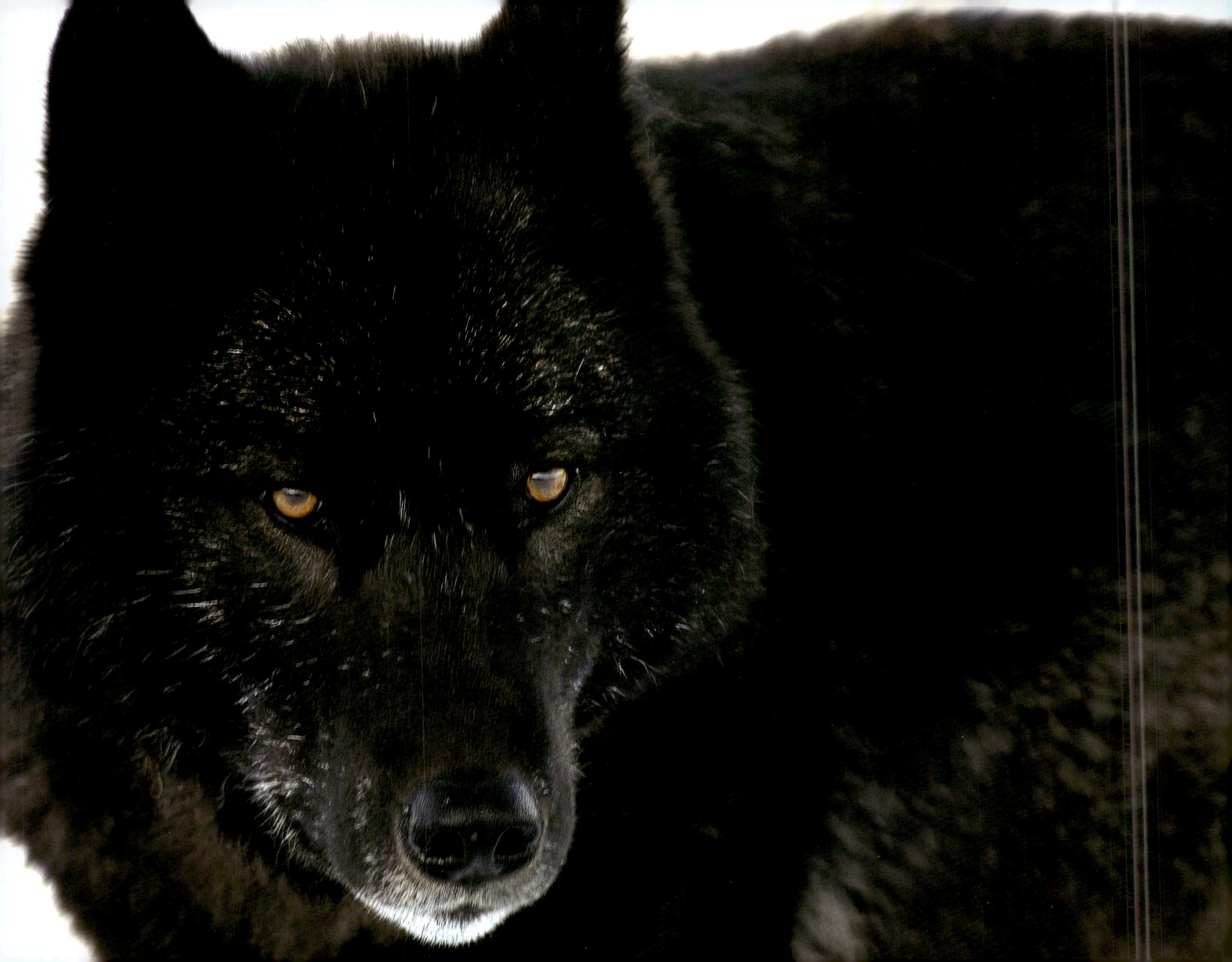

A Romeo Memory

Snow Howl

The snow was falling so fast and hard that it seemed we both might drown. Romeo stood on the lake, howling over and over into that swirling mass of white as I knelt behind my tripod maybe 30 feet away, darkness closing fast. Just then, there was no one else in the universe.

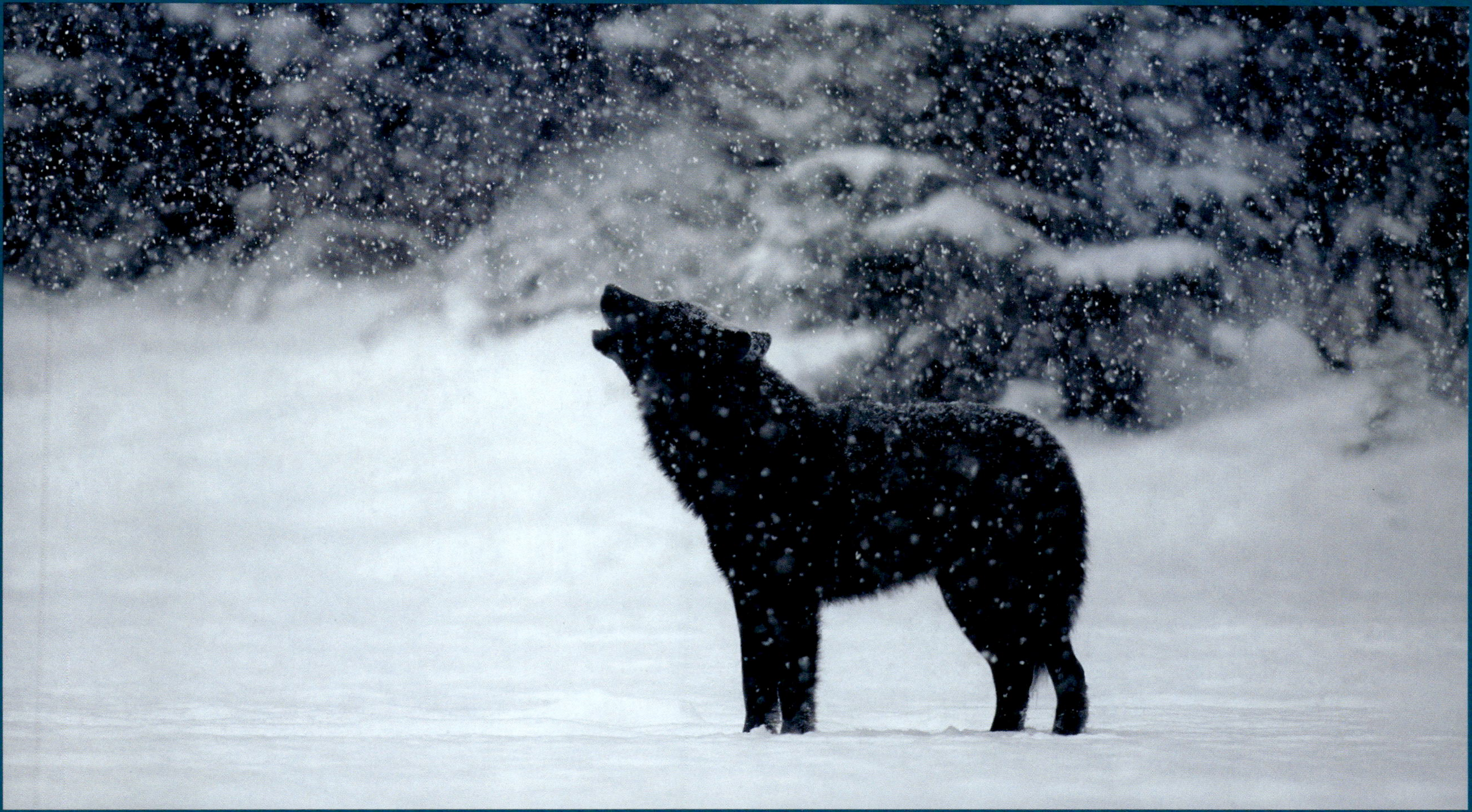

Separate from the riddle of his origins, here was a wolf, a social creature without a pack; and our dogs seemed his chosen surrogates.

That much made sense; *canis familiaris* and *canis lupus* are technically the same species, the former genetically curated descendants of their wild relatives, sharing behaviors and fully capable of interbreeding. If the chance for face time with his domestic cousins were indeed what drew the black wolf, he couldn't have picked a better place. The 5,800-acre Mendenhall Glacier Recreation Area, with its postcard backdrop, has long attracted Juneauites in all seasons. A maze of trails braid around the lake's thicketed woodlands and abrupt, snow-streaked mountains, up to the glacier's craggy, blue-white face and margins; and once the lake freezes solid each winter, its lobed ovular shape, roughly two miles across, becomes a playground for skiers, hikers, skaters . . . and of course, their canine companions. On any weekend day with halfway decent weather, there might be several dozen dogs from all ends of Juneau's coast-hugging, fifty-mile-long sprawl, coming and going in all directions—mixes and purebreds, lapdogs to coursing hounds, many of them off leash, romping with their humans and each other. And any day of the week there were neighborhood regulars out there, including us and our pack of three.

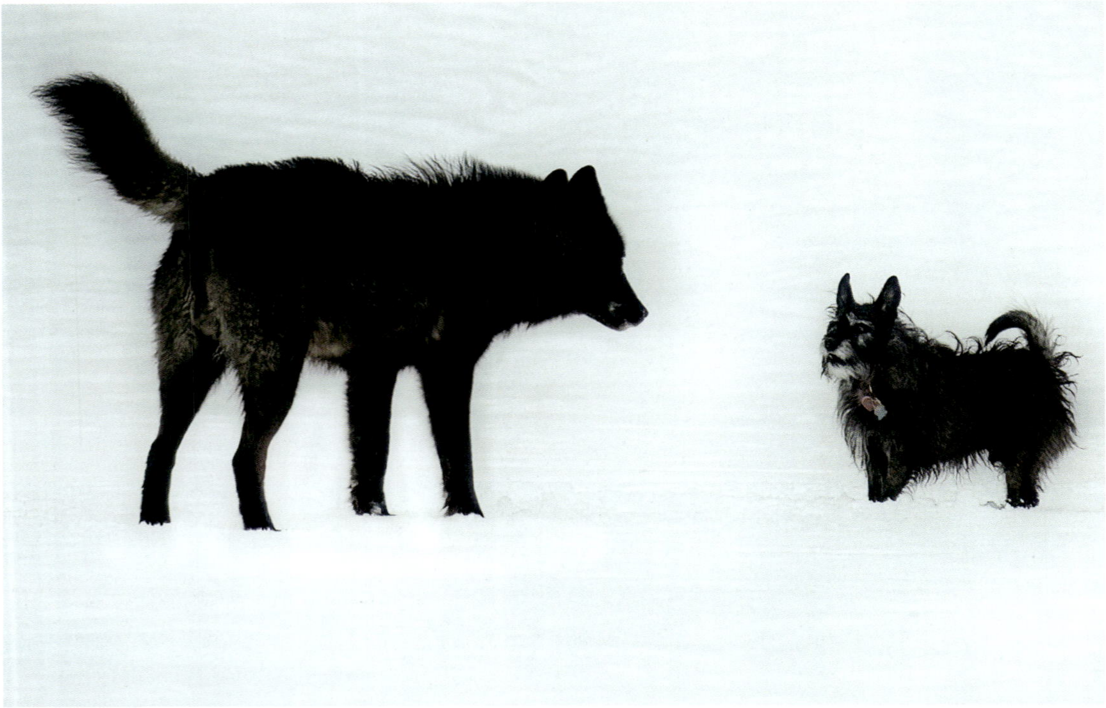

Romeo, seeming to offer condolences to one of our experiments . . .

A Romeo Memory

Superdog

Whenever any dog got close to Romeo, we were presented with an object lesson about the sheer physical difference between the two. Our retired Seeing Eye dog, Gus, was an average-sized male Labrador retriever. He looks like a junior high kid standing next to LeBron James; the wolf's head and neck match the size of his torso.

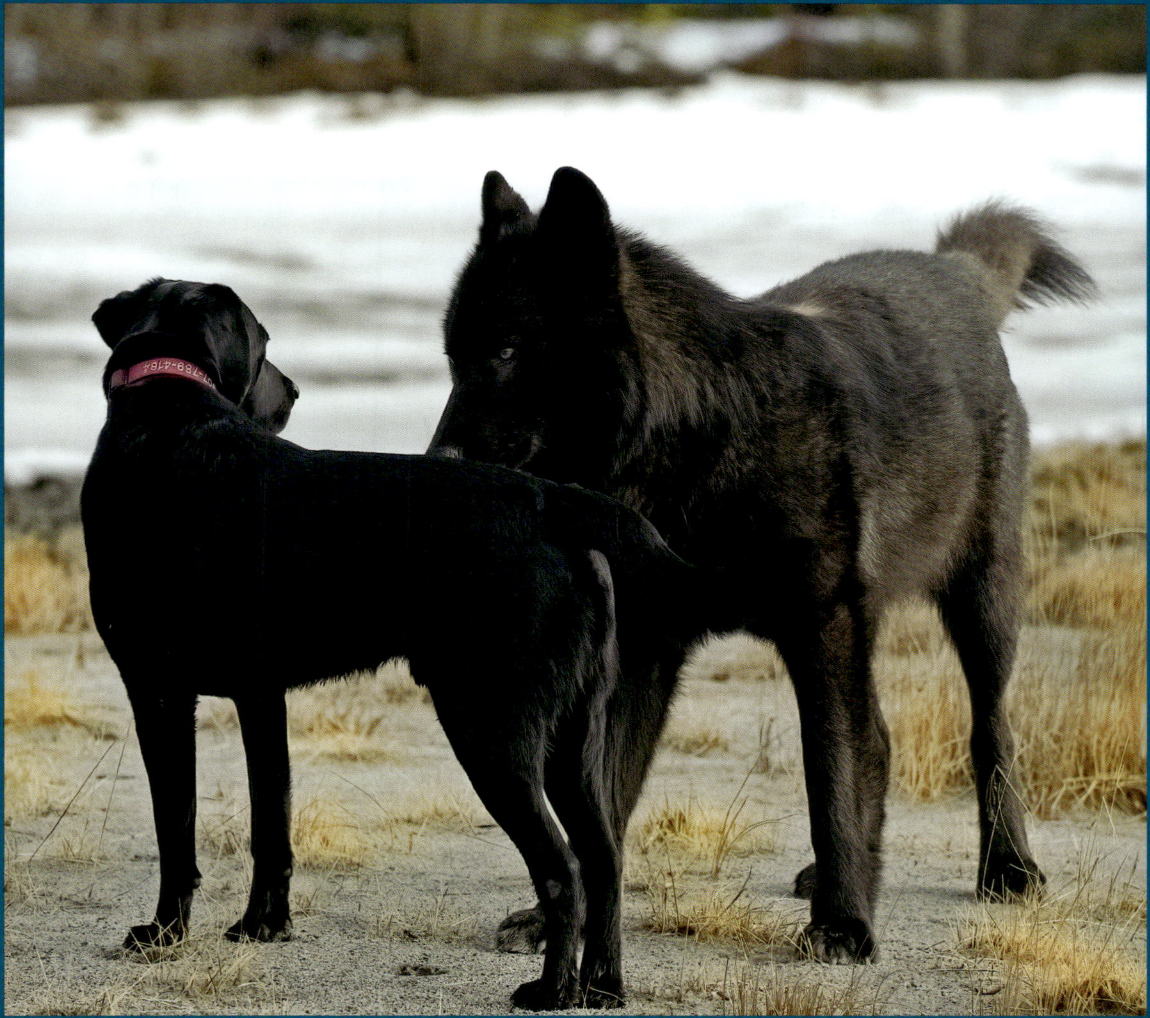

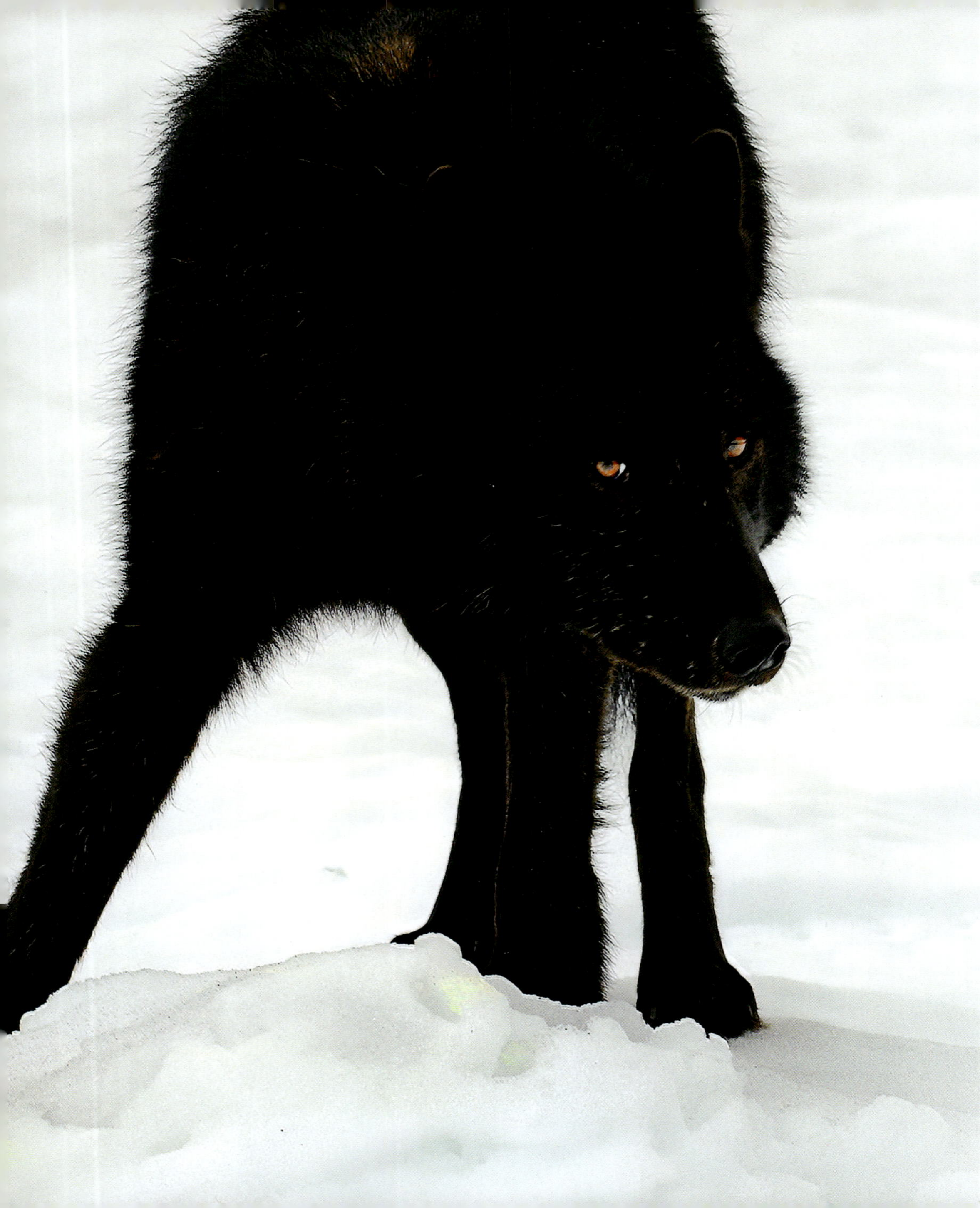

Not only was this black wolf staying put; with increasing confidence and frequency he was approaching dogs and their humans.

Tail up, ears held narrow, at times whining hysterically, he radiated an un-wolflike, nonthreatening vibe. If people banged ski poles, hurled snowballs, or dogs raised hackles, he backed off; but the next day, there he was again. If everyone were agreeable, some sort of social interchange would take place, from sniffing and traded pee-mails to all-out play sessions, punctuated by bursts of a distinctly lupine, weightless ballet that a few dogs recognized and joined. He'd watch us playing fetch, and occasionally dart in to snatch and make off with a ball. Or he trotted along at a distance, content to keep our company, a living reminder of the convoluted, sometimes bitter connection between human, wolf, and dog. After all, scant genetic distance—less than two percentage points of DNA— lies between our best friend and our darkest fear.

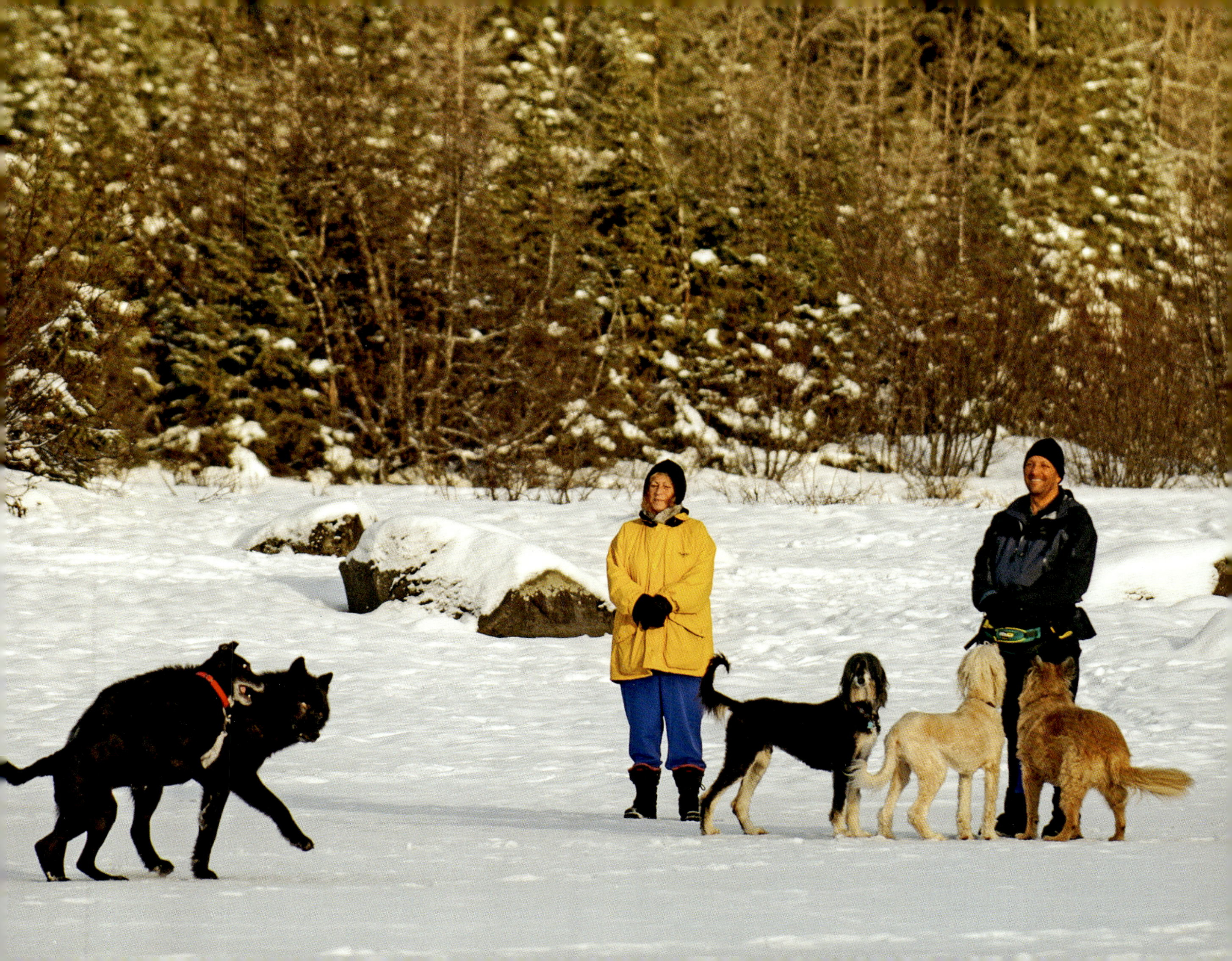

Keeping a black wolf hidden in plain sight was impossible; even less so the distinctive tracks crisscrossing the lake and echoing howls announcing his presence.

Word spread outward like ripples from a tossed stone . . . *there's a wolf out by the Mendenhall!* As the winter days lengthened, the wolf became ever more familiar, laying claim to a territory that overlapped the Capital City's most popular recreation area, not to mention adjoining yards. An increasing flow of wildlife lovers, photographers, naturalists, and the merely curious added to the usual skiers and dogwalkers; seldom more than a half dozen at any one time, but a crowd by glacier standards. From our house overlooking the wolf's favored ground, Sherrie and I not only held ringside seats for much of the unfolding drama; we found ourselves near its epicenter. When a picture and story broke on the front page of the *Empire*, Juneau's black wolf had officially arrived.

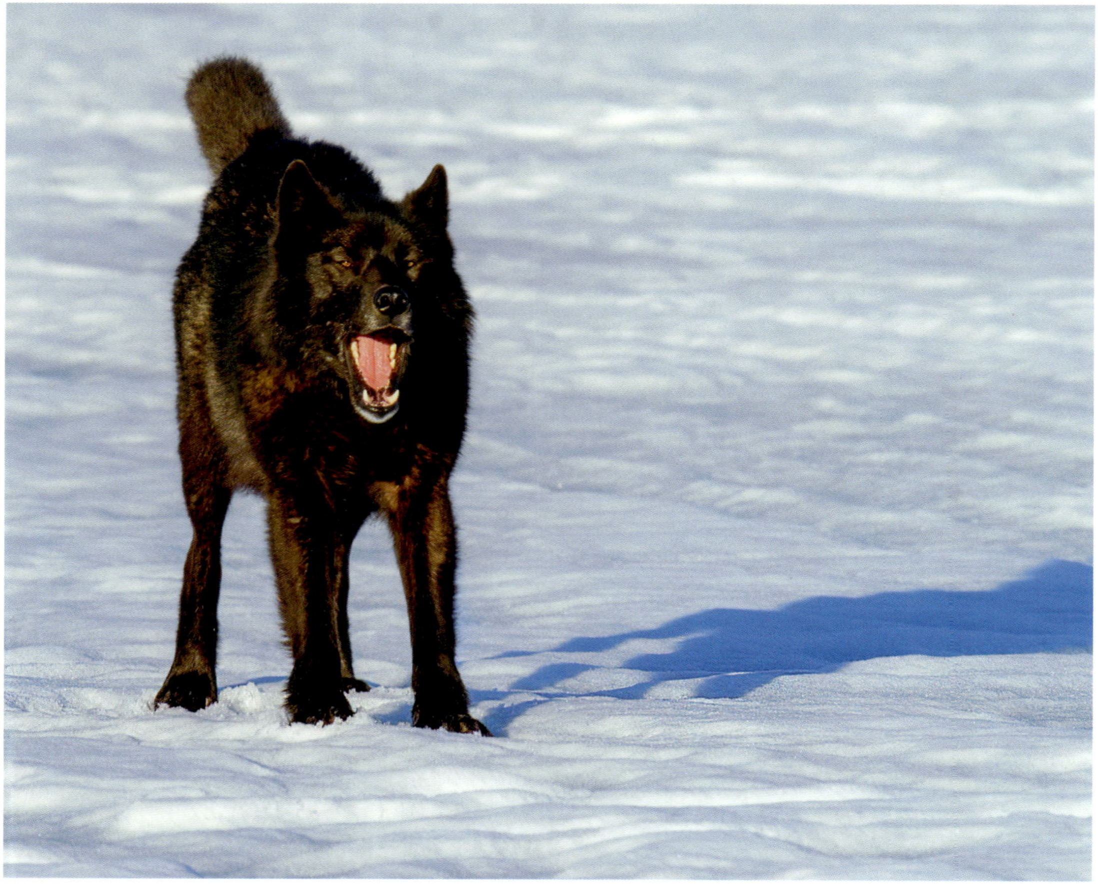

Knowledgeable locals, biologists and wildlife managers with combined centuries of wolf experience offered plausible, overlapping theories about his origins: lone survivor of a trap-decimated pack in nearby Nugget Basin; far-ranging disperser; widower or grown pup of a pregnant black female that had been struck by a taxi on Back Loop Road. Keying on his perfect teeth, gangly physique and goofy demeanor, everyone agreed this was a young wolf, probably in his second or third year. Though the details would remain a mystery, we faced one undeniable fact: the Capital City's boundaries were suddenly redefined by a living, howling emissary of the wild.

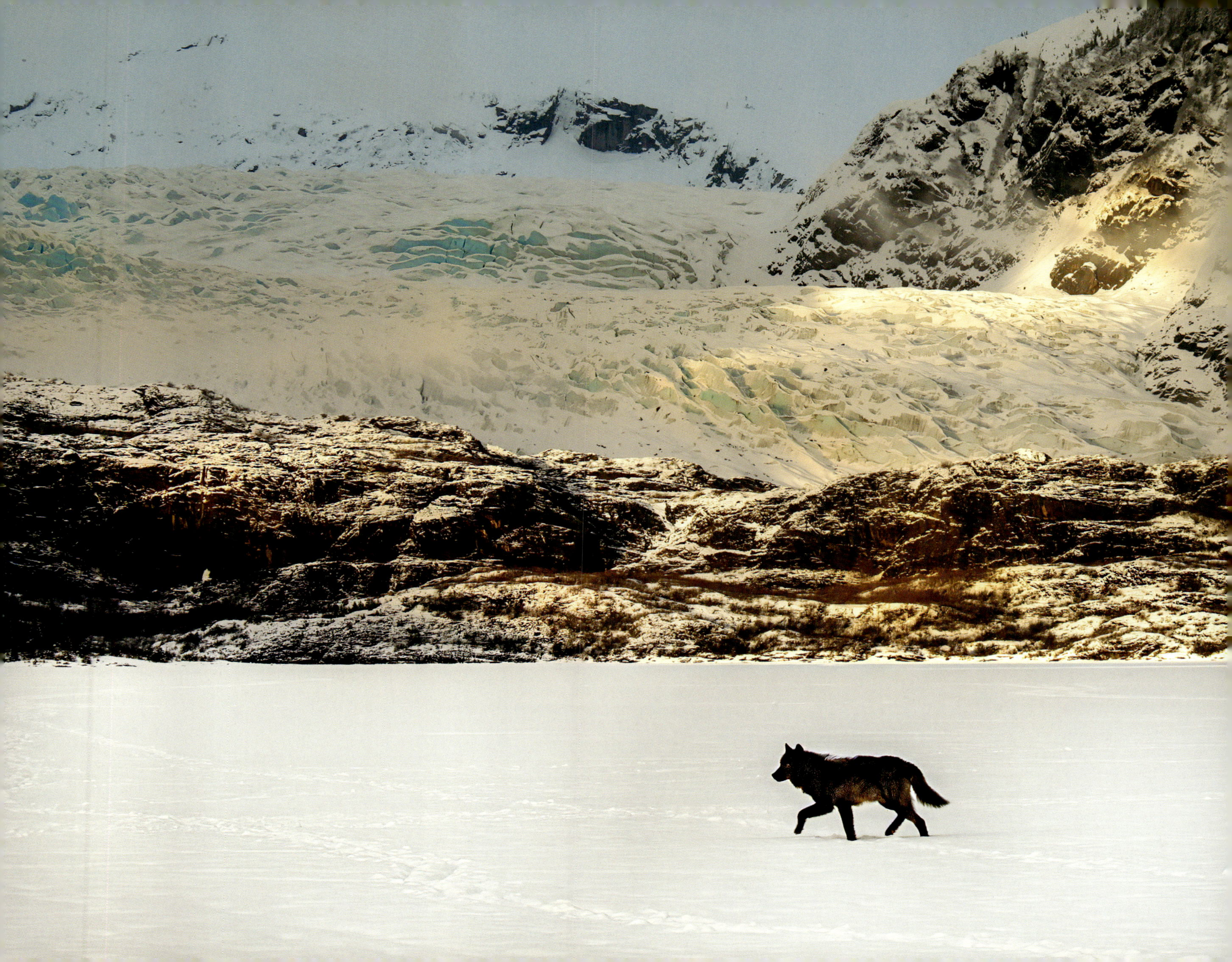

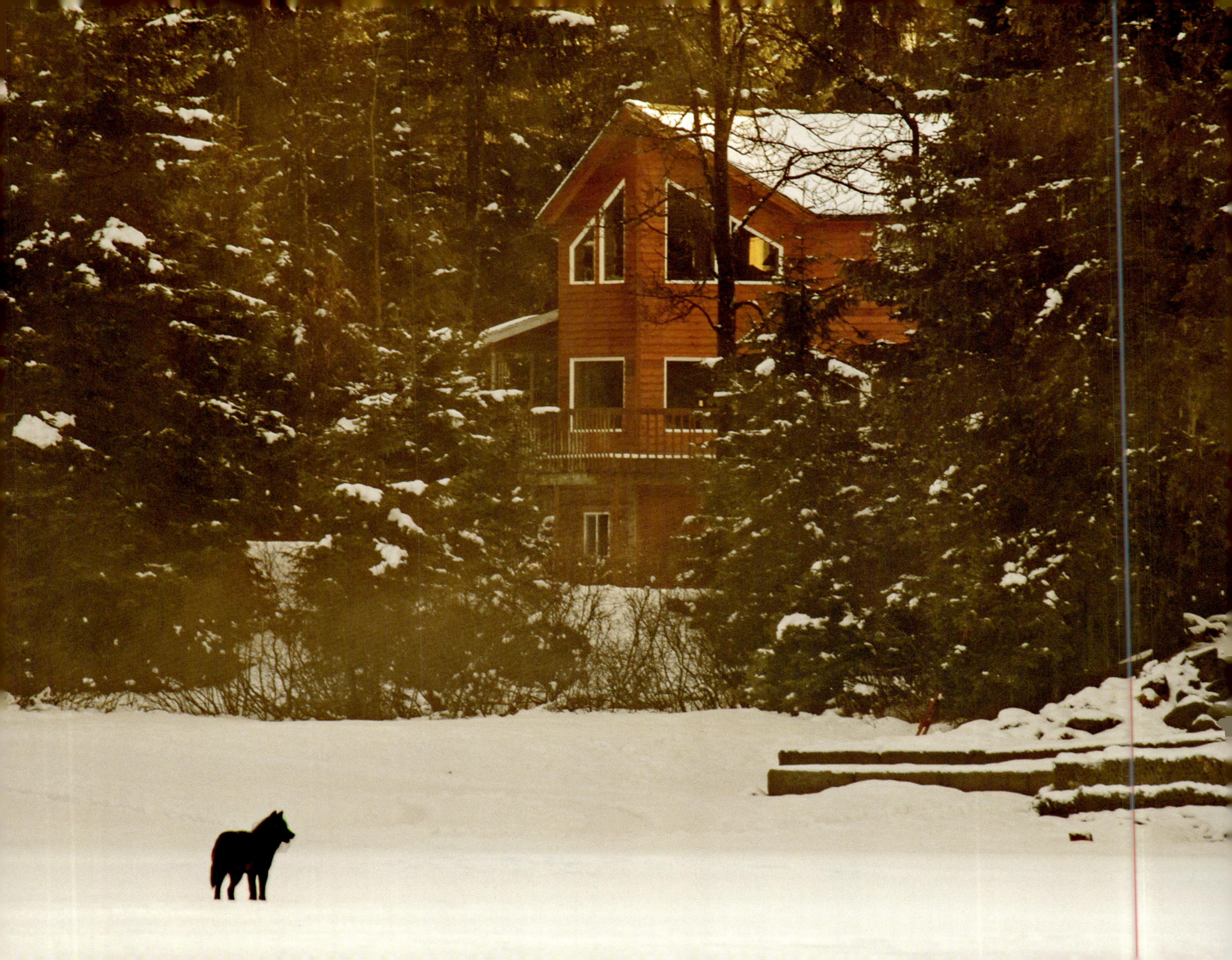

For those of us who lived within the shadow of the glacier, the expression, 'a wolf at the door,' took on literal meaning.

We sometimes found his tracks on the edge of our yard. Late at night I'd wake to his echoing howls, sometimes so close he seemed inside. With the lake as our extended yard, we could scarcely avoid encounters. He took a definite shine to Dakotah, our spayed, nine-year-old female—seeking her out, fawning and flirting, begging to play. Just past dawn one winter morning, he waited on the ice for her and the others to emerge and answer nature's call, as sooner or later they must; Sherrie, arms crossed, looked out at his curled form on the ice beyond Skaters Cabin and murmured, stern as any mom peering around curtains toward her daughter's suspicious date, *Well, there's that Romeo wolf again.* In a time before social media the name spread by mouth and stuck, cementing both his identity and a place among us.

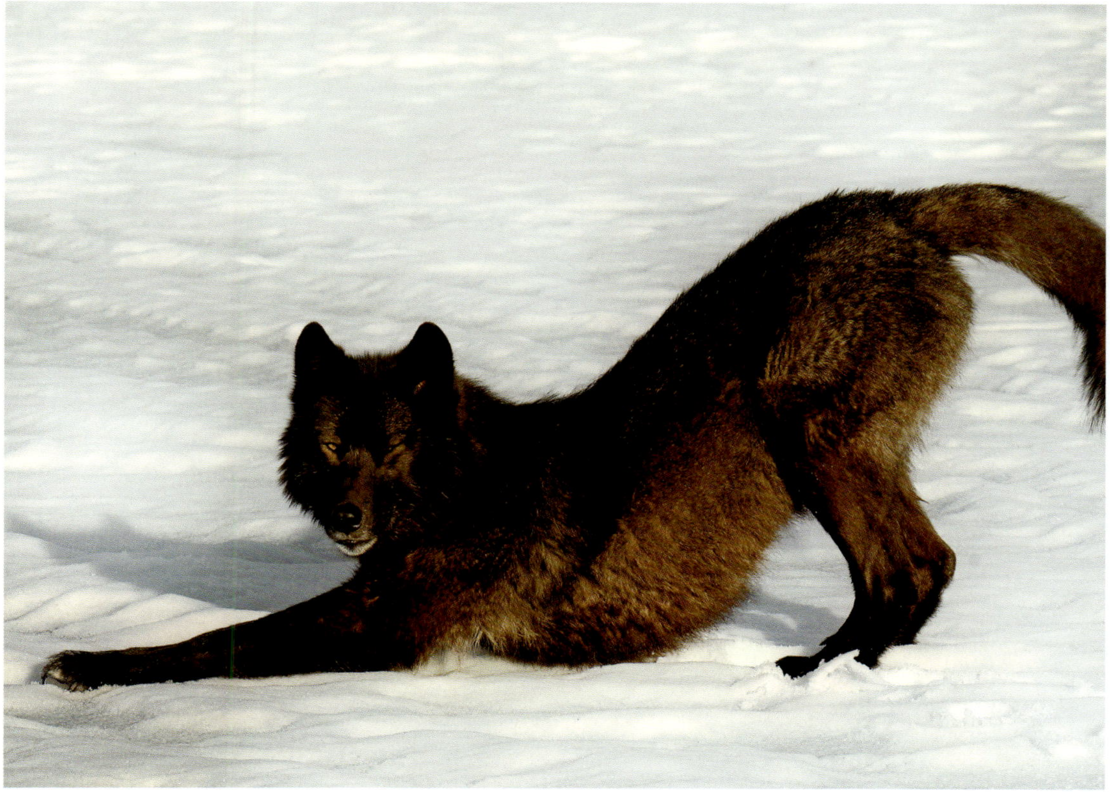

Waiting at our house . . .

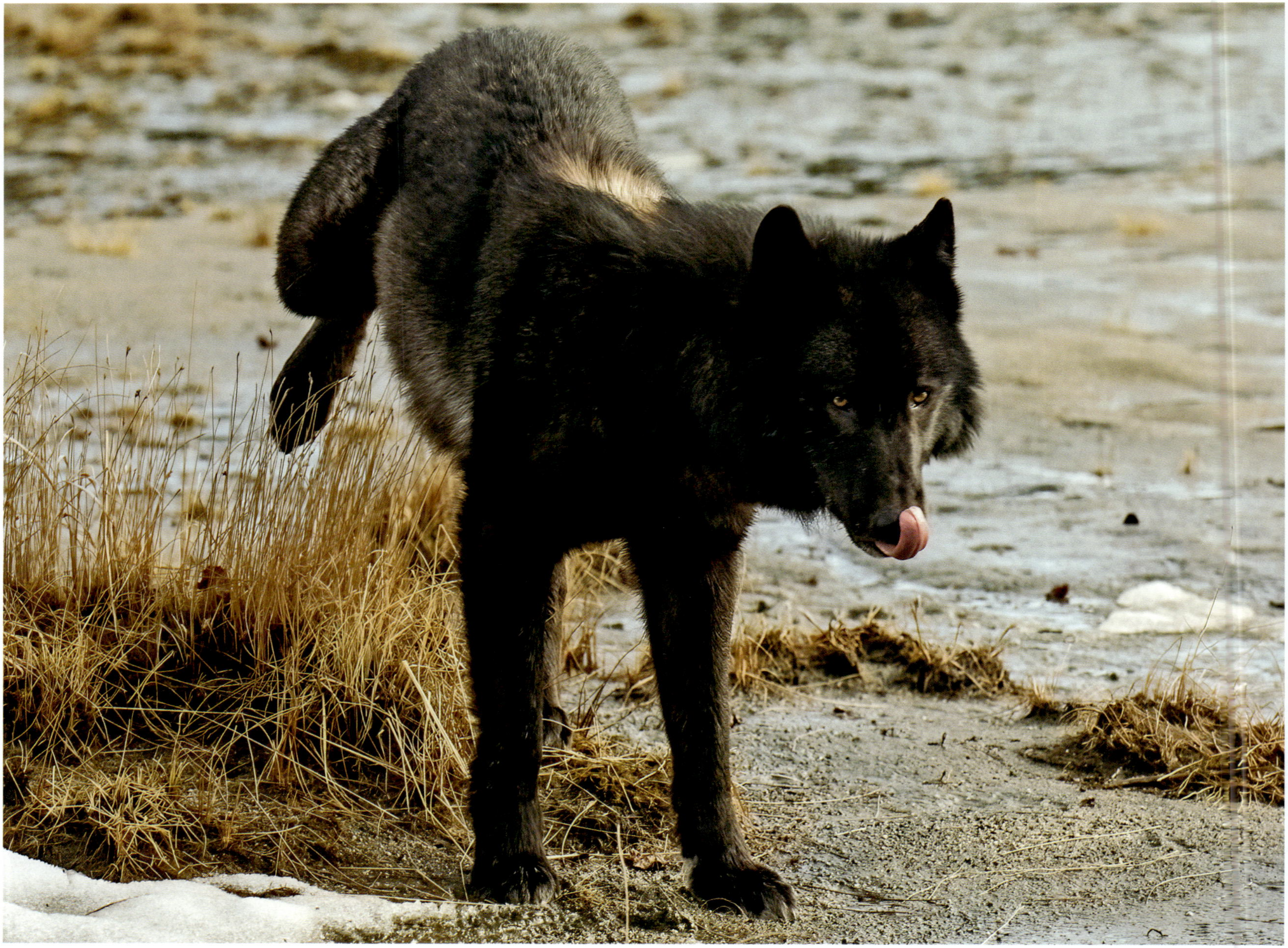

A Romeo Memory

The Power of One

Never underestimate the power of a single animal to transform a landscape. The Mendenhall Glacier and surrounding mountains may be dramatic but add a single wolf and they're utterly redefined. For six years, Romeo's presence filled the upper Mendenhall valley to overflowing.

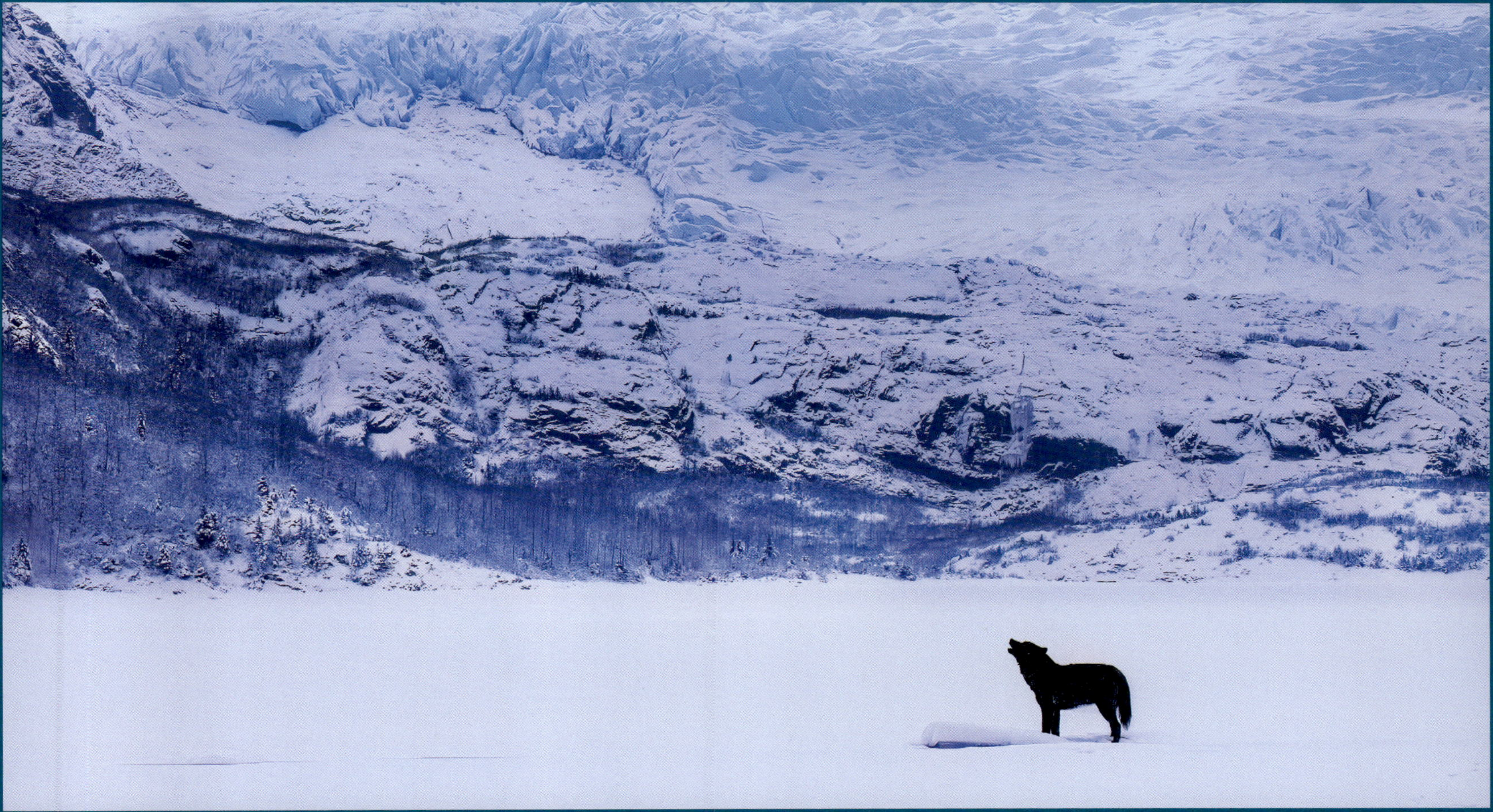

Wolf meets civilization: thirty thousand of us, one of him, and a longstanding record of wolves on the losing end.

The instant I first saw him a deep, wild thrill coursed through me, followed by a wrenching realization of the danger he faced. Sherrie, I, and a double handful of others held our collective breath. While some watched his point-blank interactions in fascination, others shook their fists. *A wolf, so close to kids, pets, and my yard?* they groused, hinting at a .44-caliber solution. Never mind that despite all the tales of menace, wolves pose less statistical threat than falling space junk. All it would take would be crossing paths with the wrong person at the wrong time, and a bullet, poison, or trap would be his end. Or maybe state biologists would decide he posed too much of a public threat and step in as they did with nuisance bears.

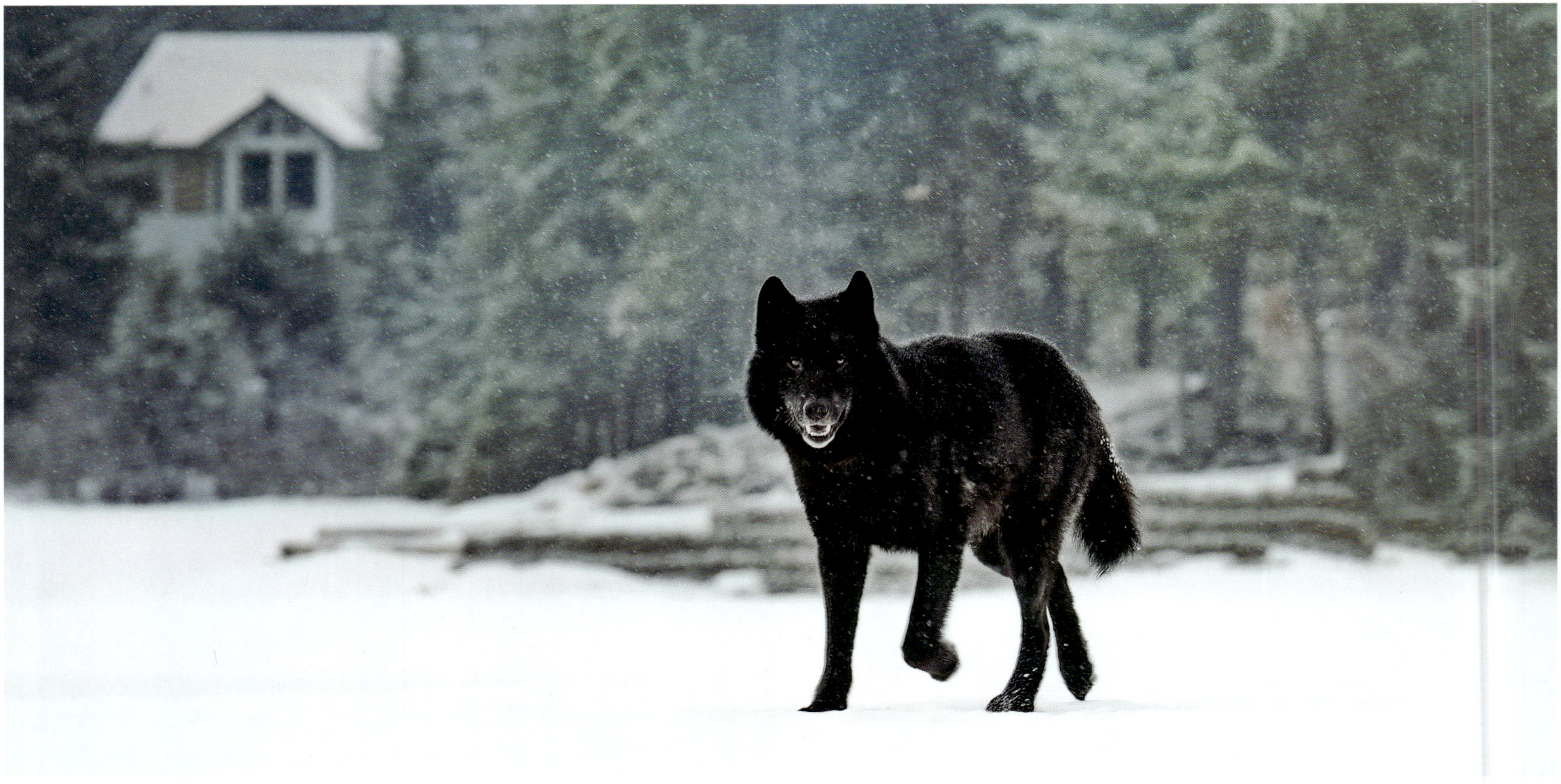

But as we all watched open-mouthed, one winter day spooled into another, spring beckoned, and the wolf we called Romeo remained.

Though one neighbor told me he'd shoot to kill if the wolf set paw in his yard, and a few locals began packing firearms on the lake, no one pulled a trigger; state and federal managers, who shared overlapping jurisdiction over the glacier area, stepped back, bemused as any of us. This Romeo wolf wasn't causing trouble, aside from making off with an occasional dog toy; in fact, he seemed better mannered than some of the mutts and people he met. He also seemed to be evolving socially, both learning and helping to create our interspecies rules of engagement. Using the local web of trails, he moved about, hunting beavers, hares, and other small game; scent-marking his territory; meeting dogs—and in the process, us as well.

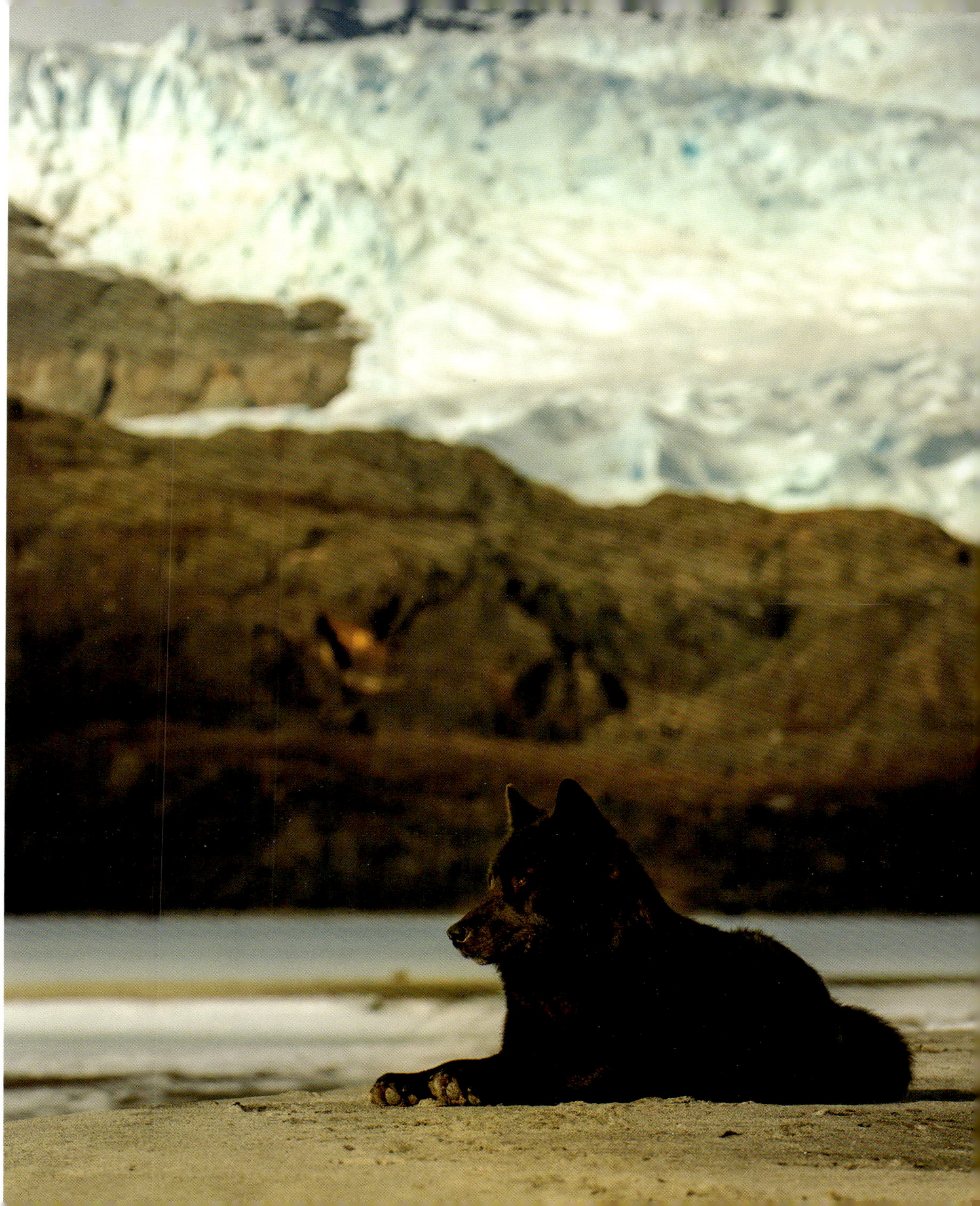

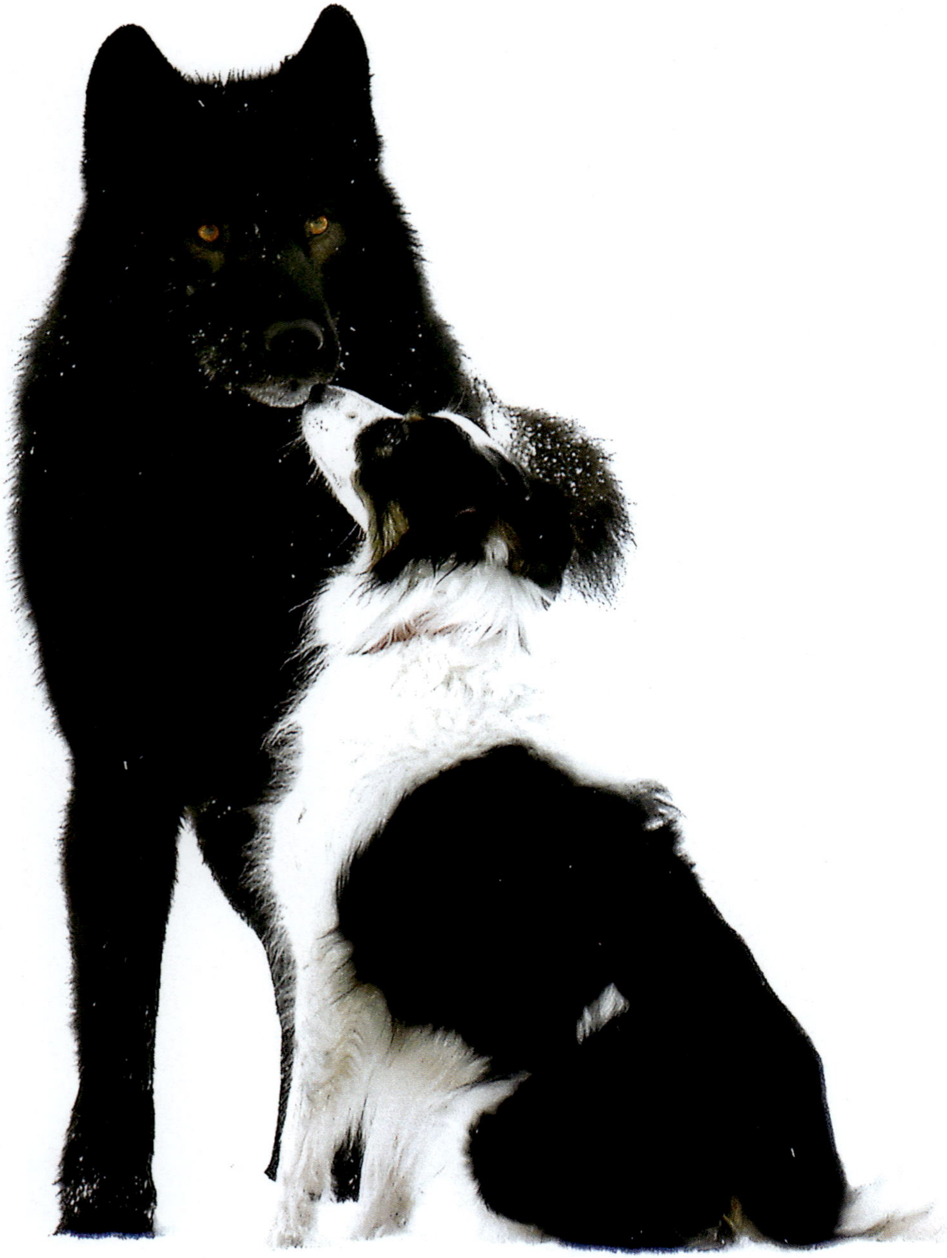

No surprise that Romeo forged close bonds with certain dogs.

He'd race across the lake to meet Jessie, our neighbor's rabbity little border collie; Dakotah, of course; Sugar, our friend Anita's big black goofball male; and Brittain, another spayed female belonging to a tall, quiet guy named Harry Robinson, to name a few. But in the process, he couldn't avoid spending time around their humans. He learned to recognize individuals at a distance and formed attachments with some, radiating body language, expressions, and behavior that eclipsed mere tolerance. He wasn't being fed nor touched; had no apparent motive to make such gestures other than that social connection we call friendship—enjoying the company of another for its own sake, a shared trait between our species.

(Left) Romeo and Jessie
(Right) Romeo following Dakotah and Sugar toward Anita

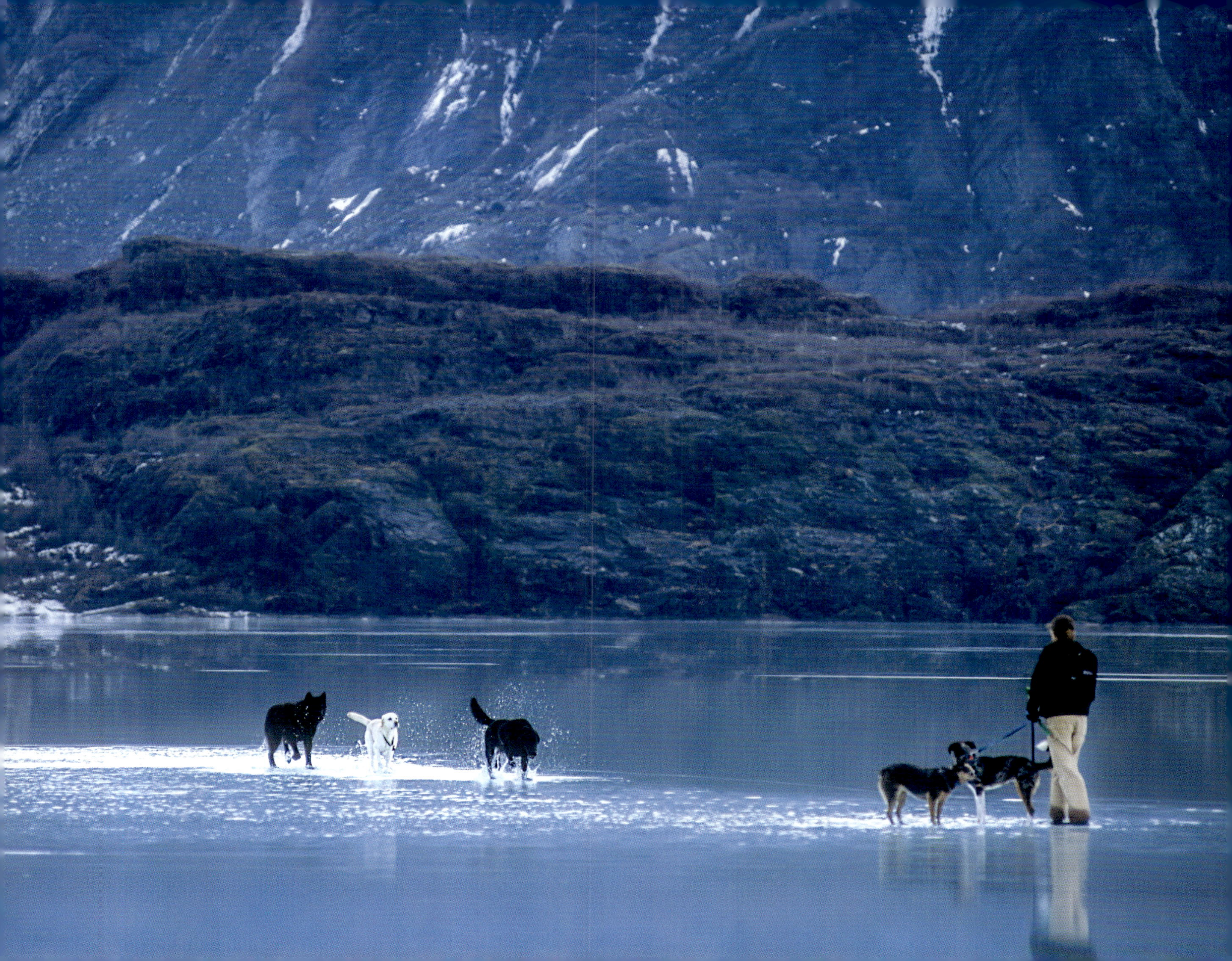

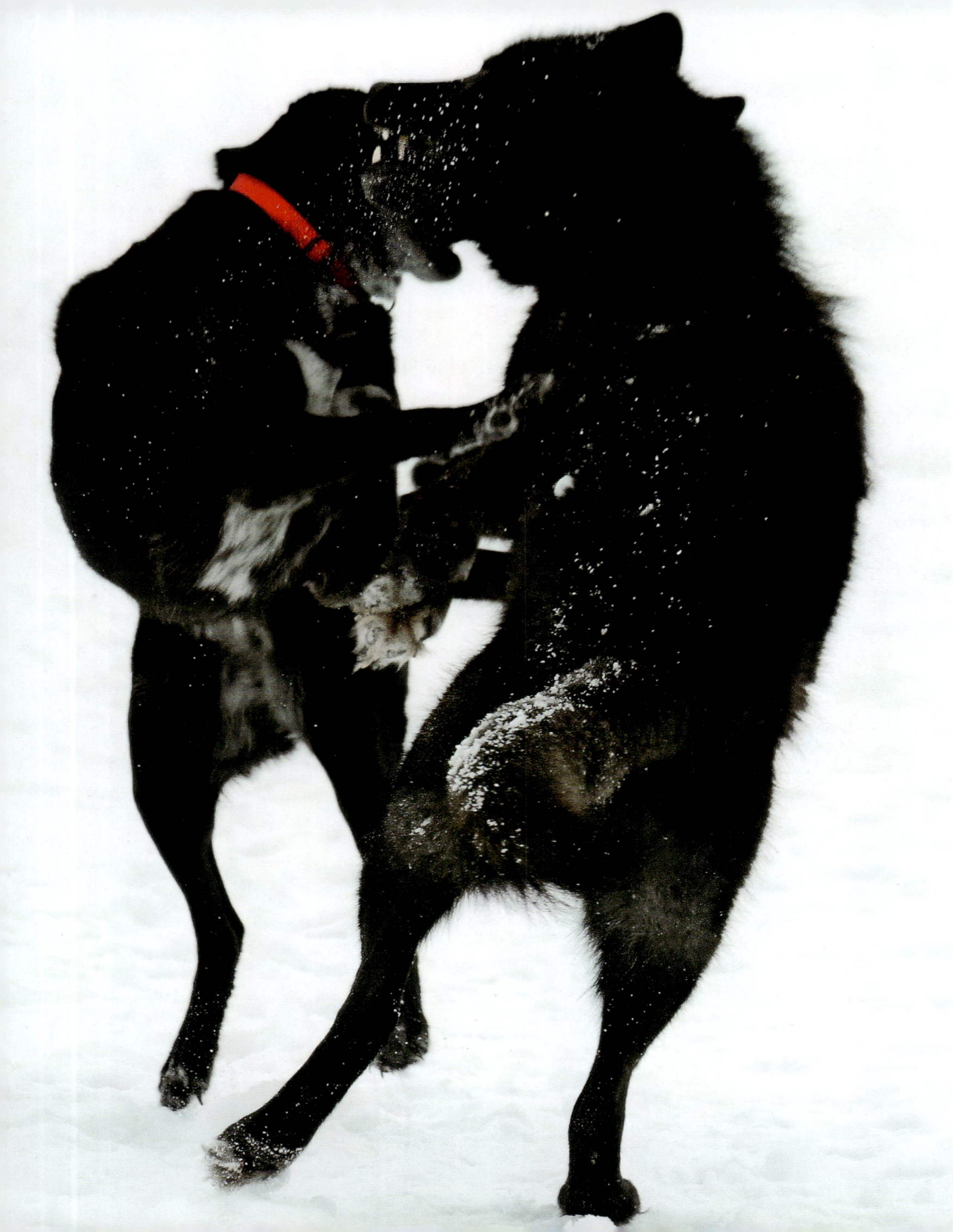

Among that group, perhaps a couple dozen in all, Harry Robinson's bond with the wolf stands out.

Harry and Brittain first met Romeo about the same time we had. Dog and wolf hit it off from the start and Harry, with a deep empathy for animals, followed the flow. Soon he, Brittain, and Romeo were meeting daily and taking miles-long hikes punctuated by play sessions; the wolf would often be waiting for their arrival at a trailhead parking lot, and if he didn't appear, Harry would howl—with a poor accent, he'd admit—and Romeo, if in earshot, would come at a dead run. Over weeks, then months, the closeness between Brittain and the wolf radiated outward to include Harry. On meeting, Romeo would focus on him as well as Brittain, and make the sort of friendly gestures—narrowed ears, grins, relaxed, social yawns and bows—that we recognize in our own; anything a dog does, a wolf did first.

Brittain and Romeo

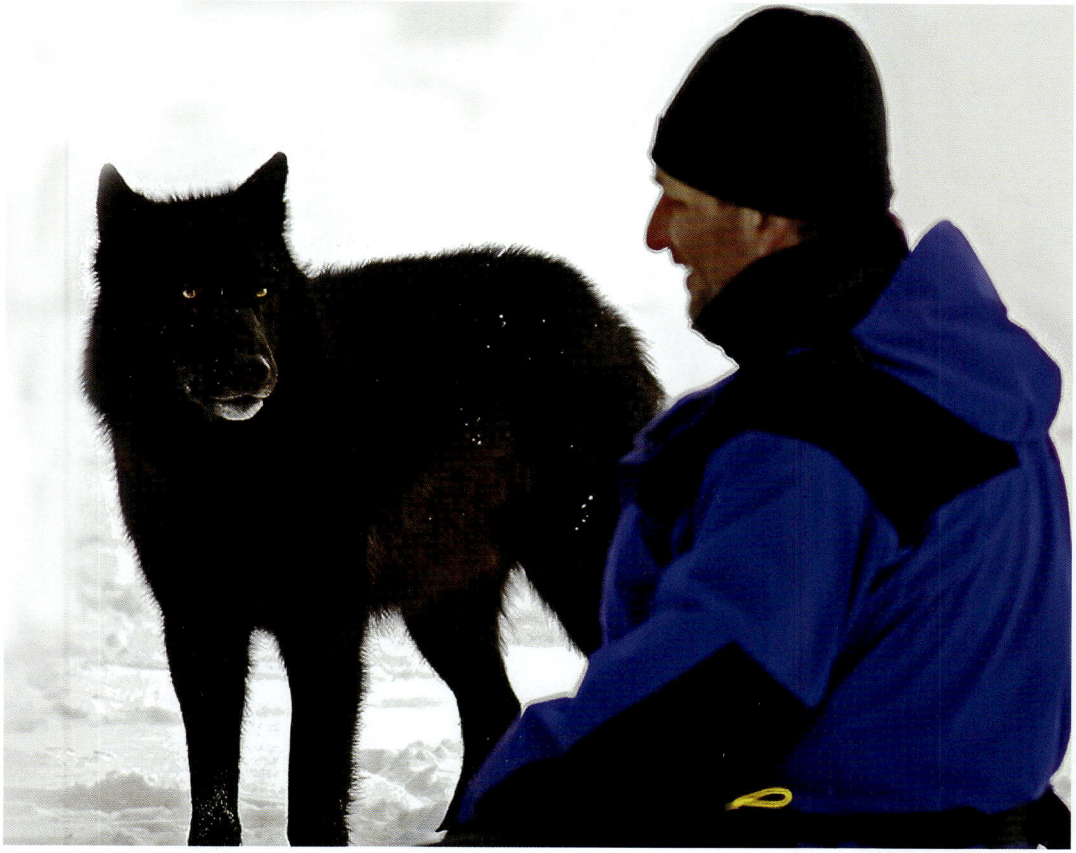

Romeo and Harry

Romeo gained no direct survival benefit from these interchanges; Harry never fed nor tried to touch the wolf, though Romeo would now and then brush against a leg as he roughhoused with Brittain or loped past on a narrow trail.

No one doubts that profound emotional connections can form between humans and dogs—in fact, are the norm; so why not between us and the domestic dog's forebear? After all, sociable wolves must have lingered by our fires not once but many times for us to sit with their muted and shaped souls at our feet.

As the bright days of April merged into May, the lake ice melted and the snow retreated uphill; and Romeo followed, fading into the glaciered mountain wilds cradling Juneau.

That was *that,* we told one another, both thrilled by the experience and relieved he'd left. But sightings and rumors of a black wolf continued—on Thunder Mountain, near Herbert River, down by Thane; and with the end of autumn Romeo appeared again out by the glacier, reuniting with friends and acquaintances, both two-and-four-legged, and attracting renewed attention.

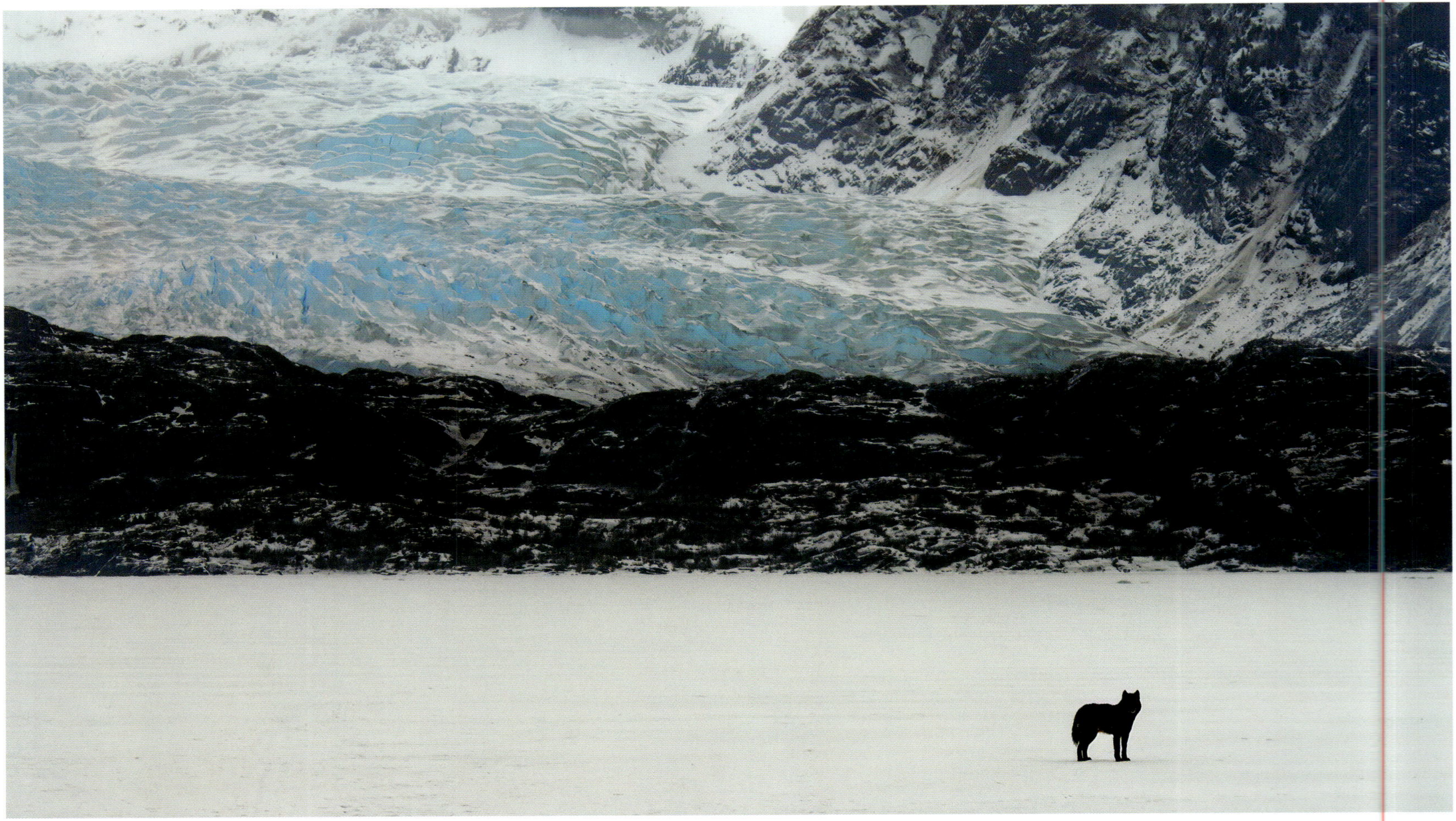

A Romeo Memory

A Nap on the Ice

It was one of those warm bright April days when winter is suddenly over. Gus and I skied out and met Romeo near the river mouth. I took off my skis and lay on the snow, head on my pack; Gus put his chin on my leg, and the wolf reclined, twenty feet away. Together, we took a nap in the sun as the snow collapsed in hisses. I still wonder at the trust that took—not on our part, but his.

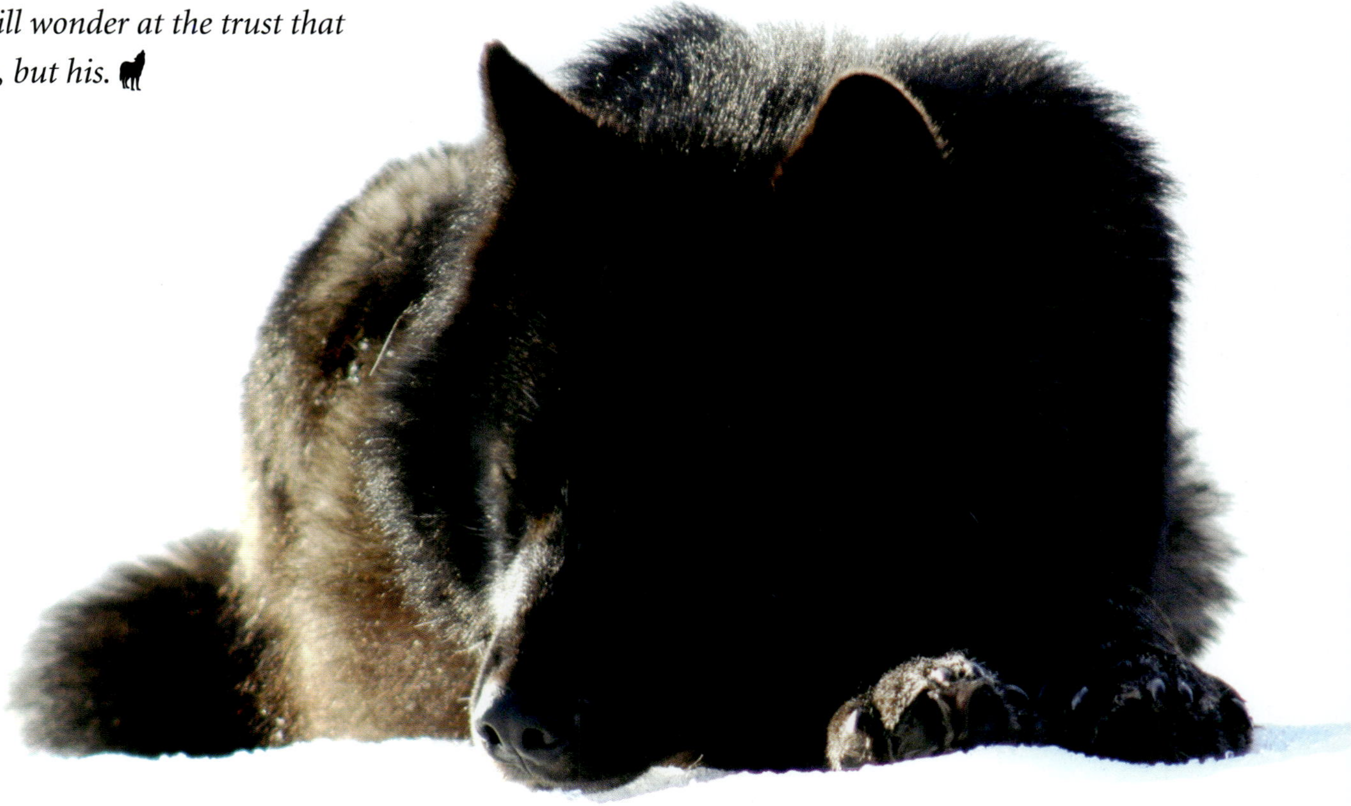

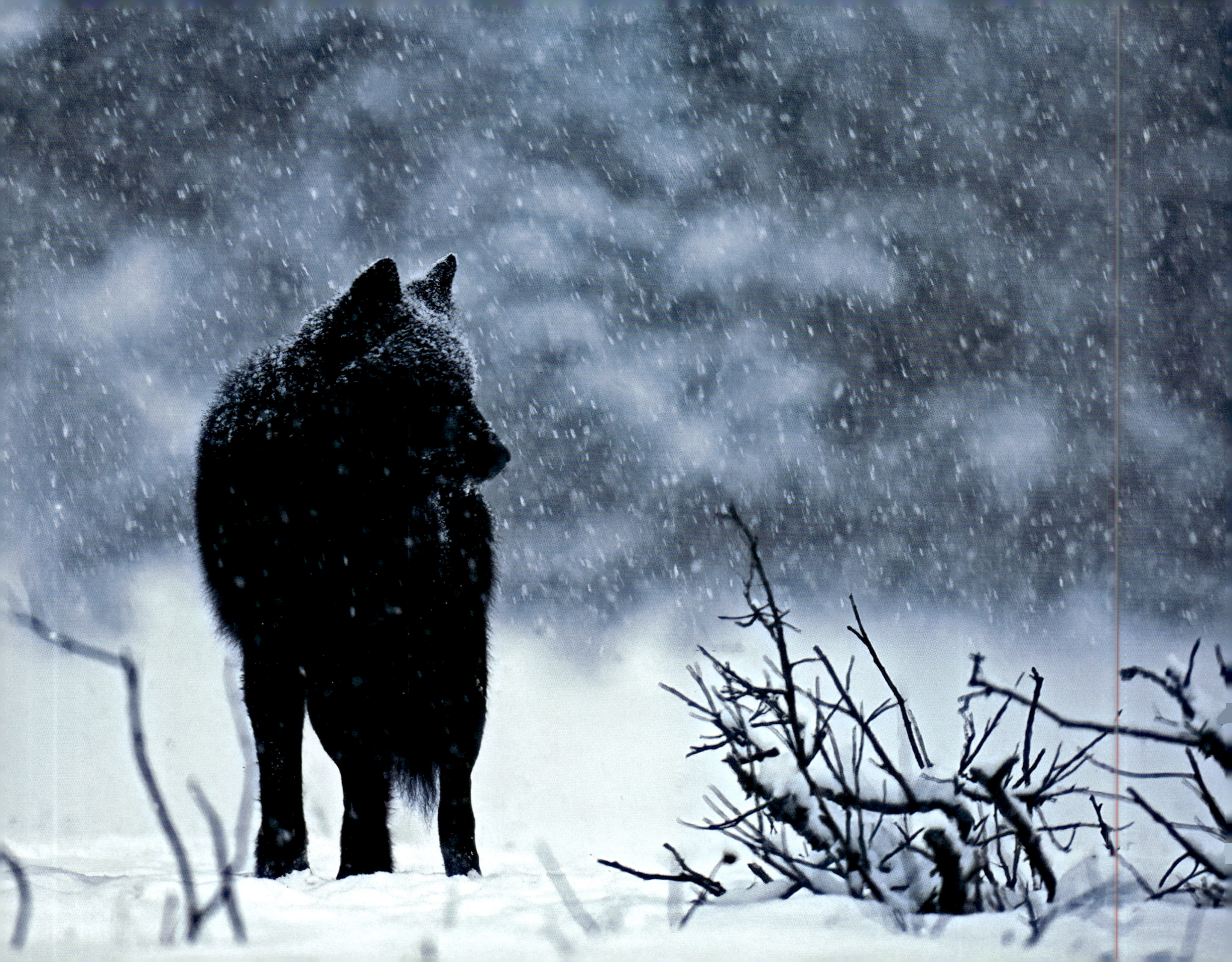

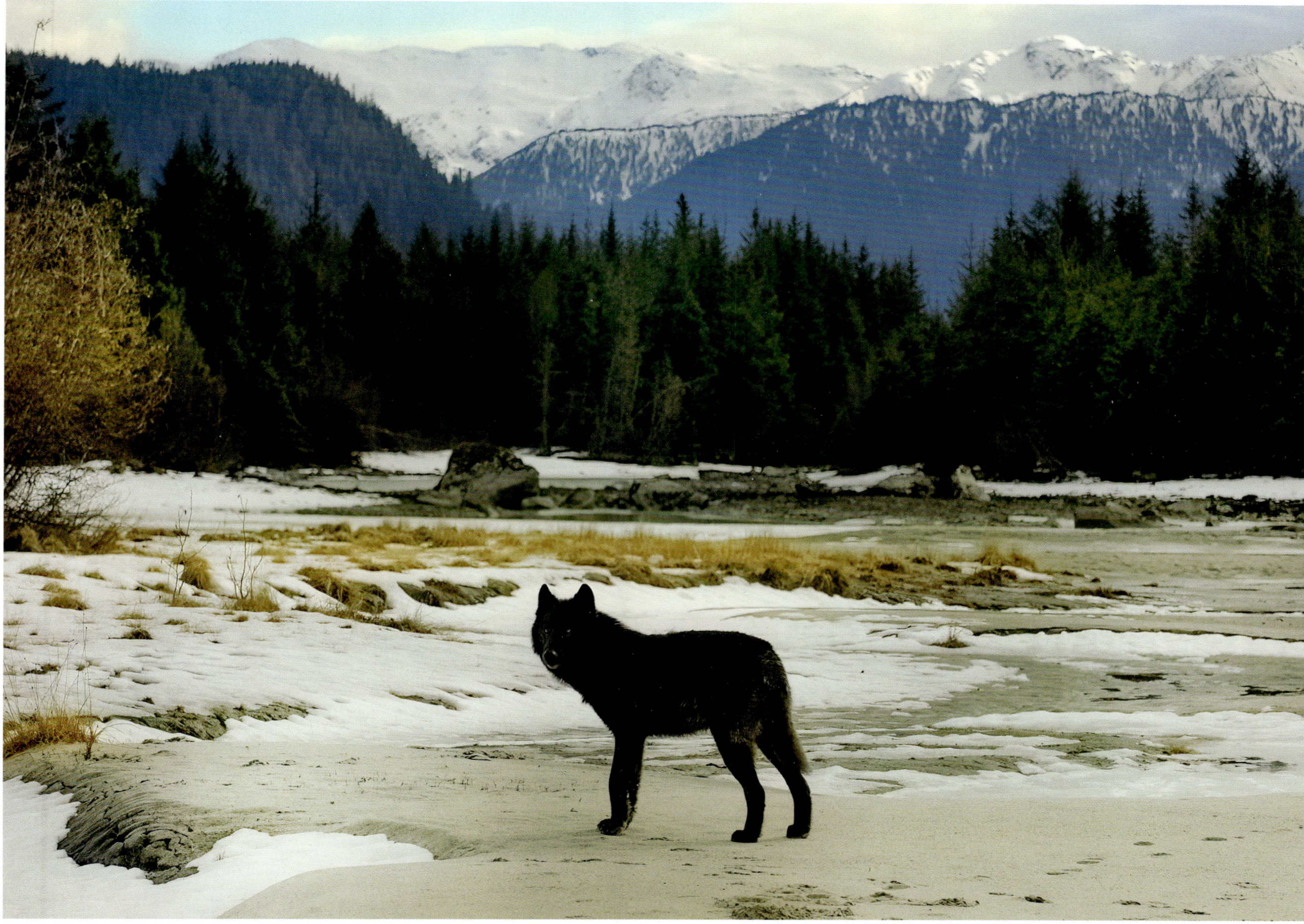

A wolf for all seasons . . .

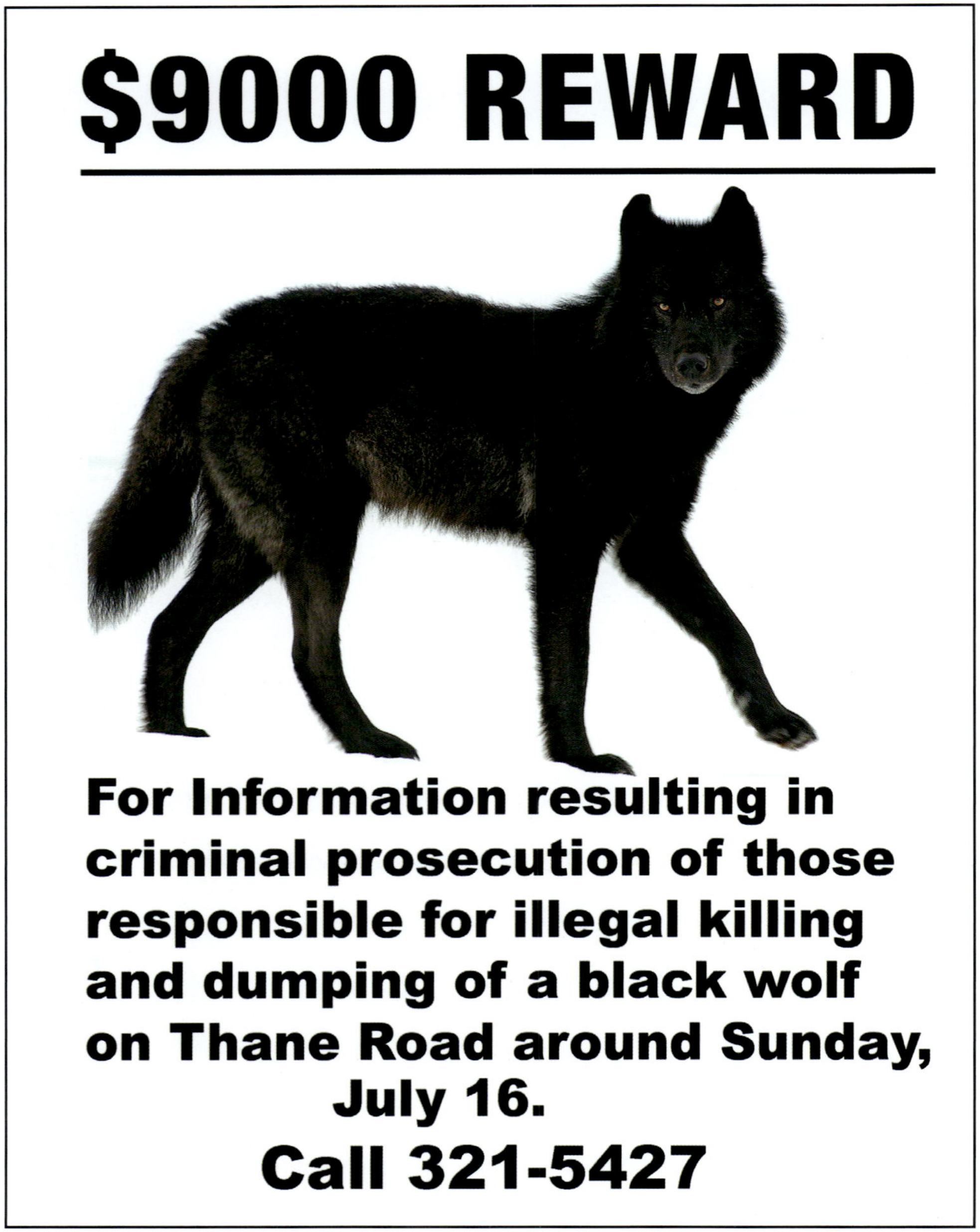

> Fame, as usual, proved double-edged. Though most Juneauites were both respectful and concerned for the wolf's well-being, Romeo was exposed at times to humans ranging from clueless to malevolent.

I saw teenagers encircling him and howling; adults taunting or encouraging conflict with aggressive, ill-mannered or even in-heat dogs (the latter, without result). People who didn't know any better pressed too close with their point-and-shoots, dogs and kids in tow; now and then he'd get buzzed by snowmobilers. Romeo took it all in stride, his day-to-day survival testament to the choices he made. If he'd so much as bared a tooth in return, he'd have been dead.

Several times, we had reason to fear the worst.

I twice overheard conversations discussing the black wolf's demise, in past tense. And in the predawn murk one winter morning, I awoke to the repeated, echoing crash of a large-caliber revolver being emptied near Skaters Cabin, where Romeo often waited for early dog walkers. In 2006, a dead, bullet-riddled black wolf was found dumped by a roadside and everyone knew it was Romeo—in fact, a community grassroots effort offered a reward that topped $10,000. But each time, Romeo rose as if from the dead; the Jesus Wolf, some called him.

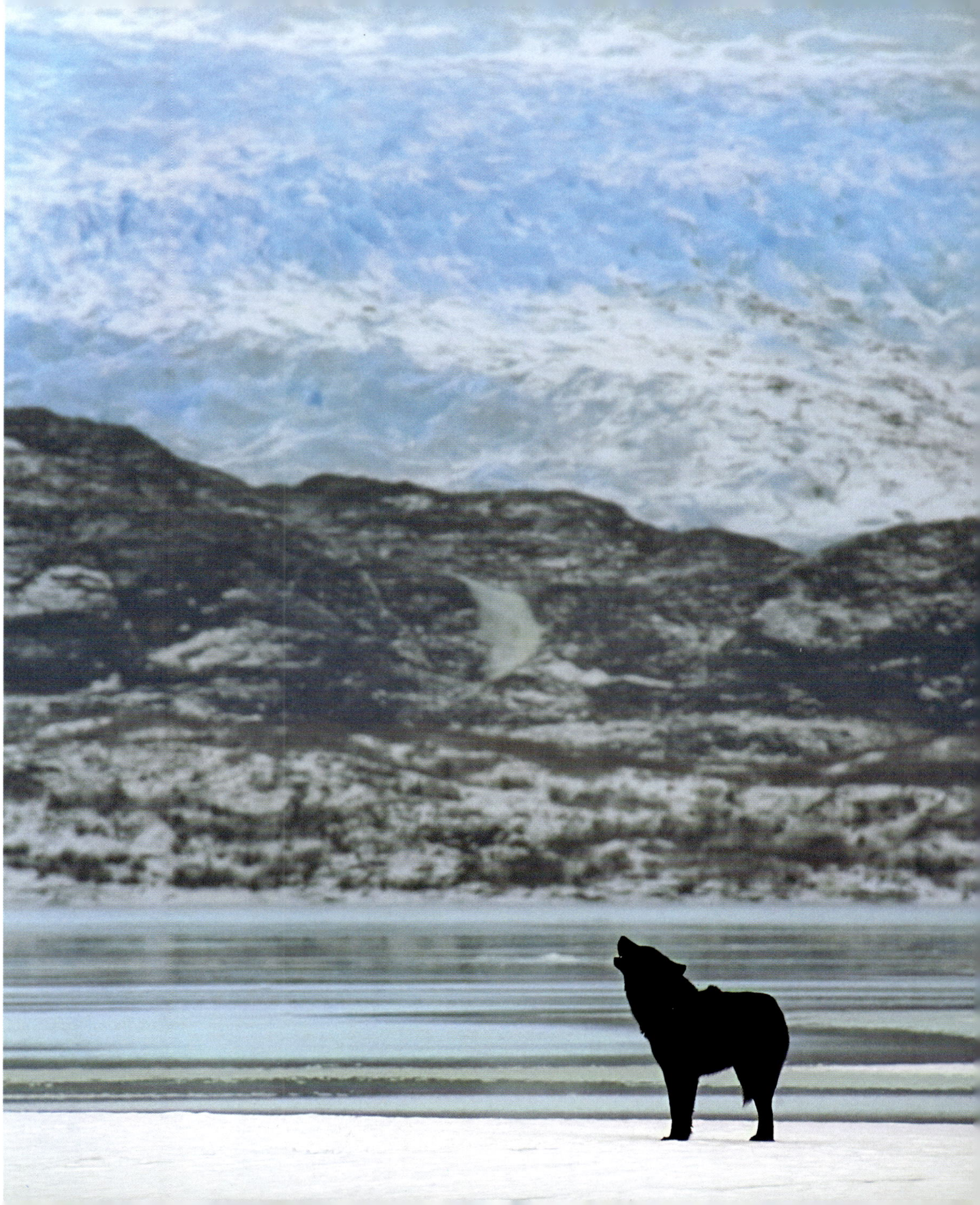

Even in a perfect world, the dozens of daily off-leash interactions between Romeo and dogs of all shapes and temperaments, with a similar range of owners, issues were inevitable.

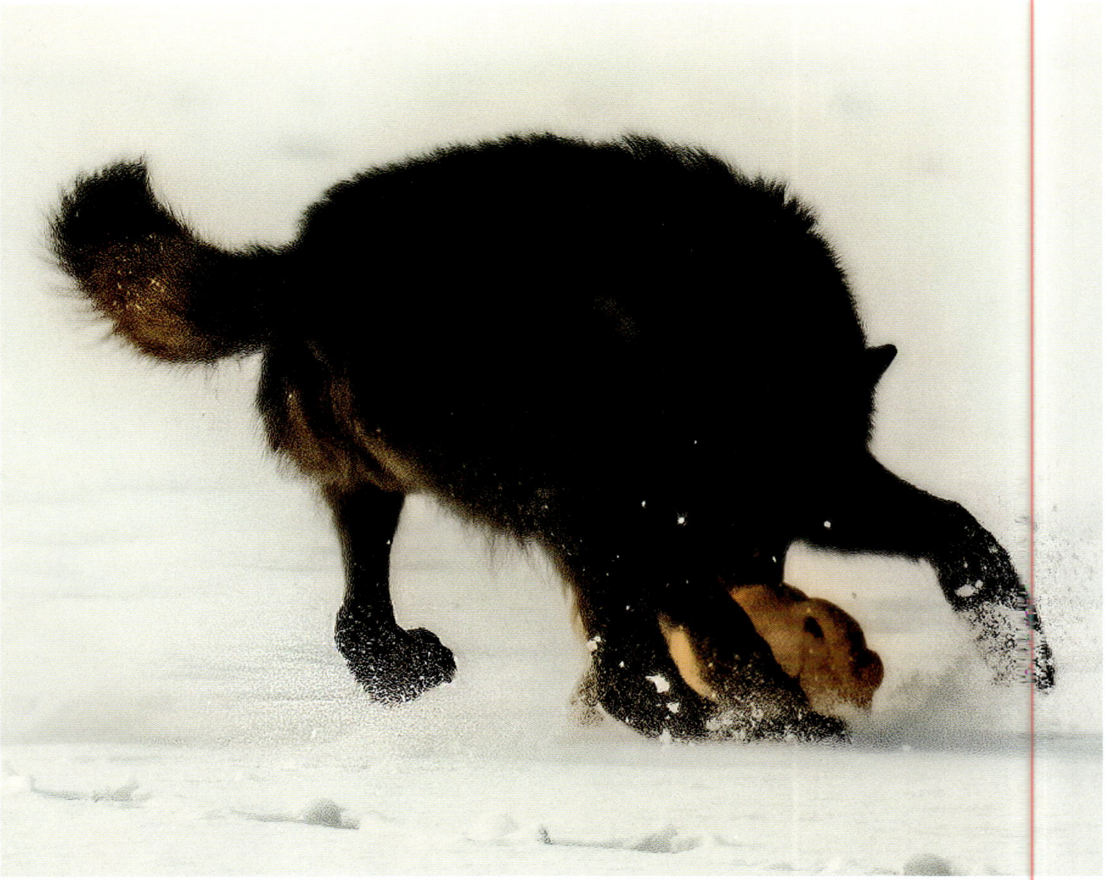

The wolf was attacked without warning by two large German Shepherds he knew, a wound on his back that took months to heal.

Capable of killing either dog, Romeo didn't retaliate. Three times he snatched small dogs and carried them by the scruff in those bone-crushing jaws, then released them without injury—as with the pug at right. And over years, three dogs, all small and off leash, vanished in circumstances that pointed to predatory activity; the only one that was witnessed was a Pomeranian, which Romeo clearly did carry off. Two owners blamed themselves; the third's demands for the wolf's removal were refused due to lack of evidence. There were sporadic, minor tiffs and incidents; considering the unsupervised thousands of close contacts between wolf, dogs, and people day in and out over years in shifting circumstances, a rather remarkable record of peaceful coexistence. Nonetheless, pressure remained on officials to *do* something. Wildlife biologists tried to haze the wolf away with shotgun-fired bean bags and cracker shells, but each time Romeo returned in a matter of days. Public pressure helped convince officials considering having the black wolf relocated or euthanized to press the pause button. And Romeo trotted on.

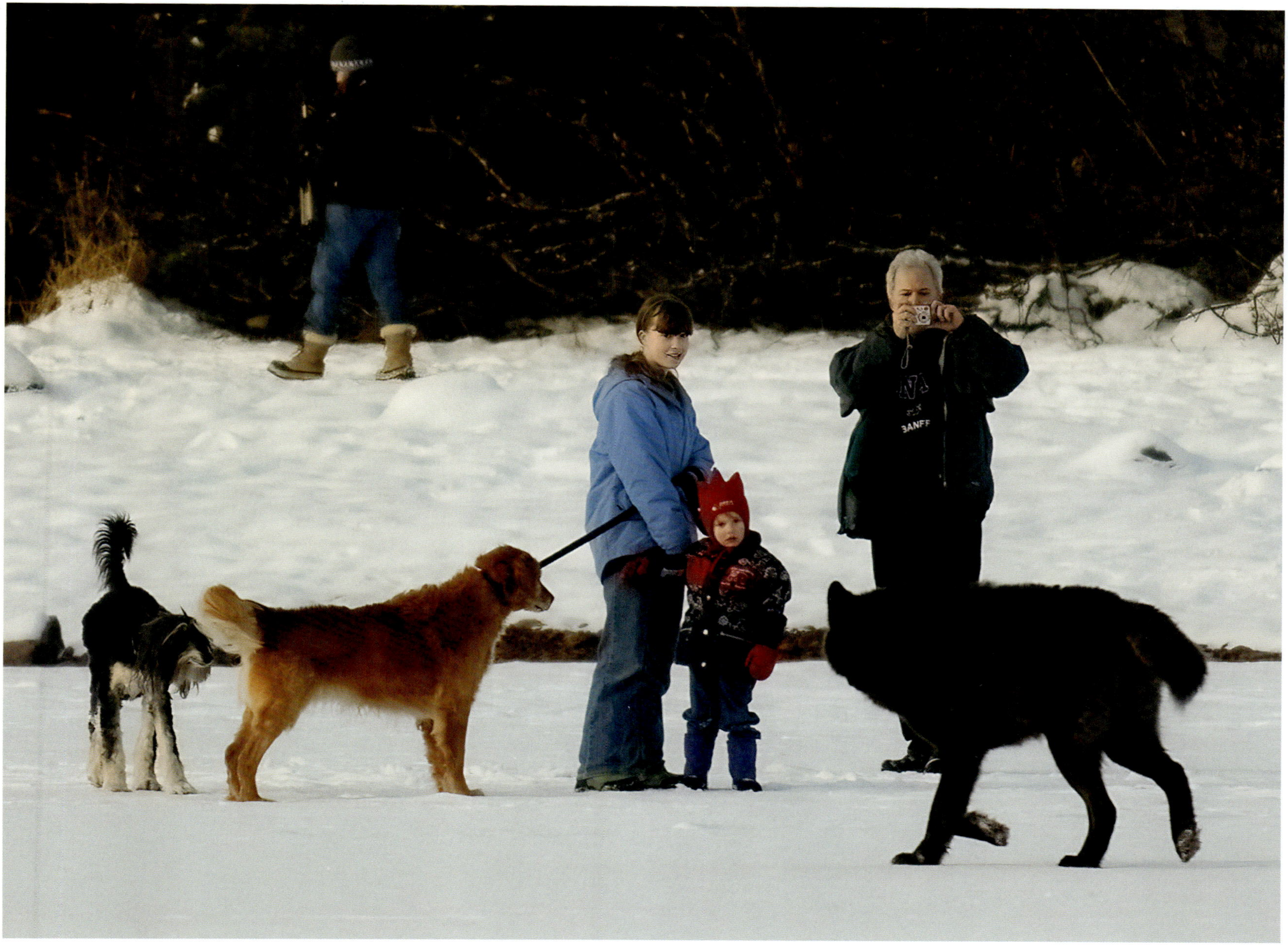

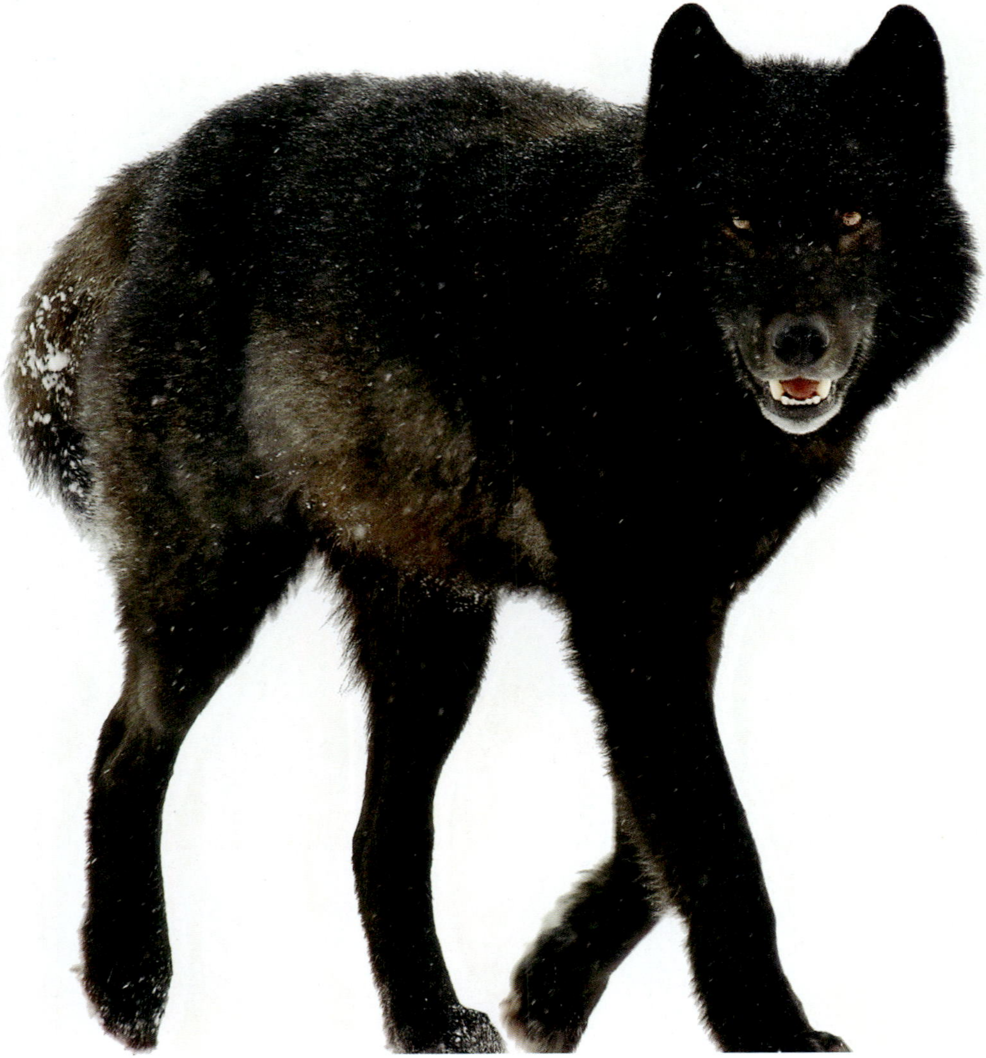

Overarching Romeo's always-tenuous presence, the issue of wolf politics loomed.

Predator control was then and remains a hot-button issue, contentious as any in the Great Land: in short, the question of killing or not killing wolves and bears—and if so, where, how, and how many—to theoretically make more moose and caribou available to human hunters. Supported more by conviction and anecdote than sound science, opposed by many Alaskans as unethical and downright distasteful, predator control had been twice curtailed by statewide ballot measures, then reinstated by the legislature. A third ballot measure was in the works; both gubernatorial administrations during Romeo's time promoted predator control, claiming it was a matter of public safety as well. And irony of ironies, less than a half hour's drive from the governor's mansion ranged a living, howling poster child for not the bad, but the Big *Good* Wolf, palling around with people and dogs, flashing his signature grin.

A Romeo Memory

Dogs, Dogs, Dogs . . .

Romeo's relationships with dogs varied to fit individuals. He bounded along with fetching Labs; roughhoused with like-minded larger canines; nuzzled elders gently; and he loved to gallop down the ice with this pair of bred-to-run Afghans.

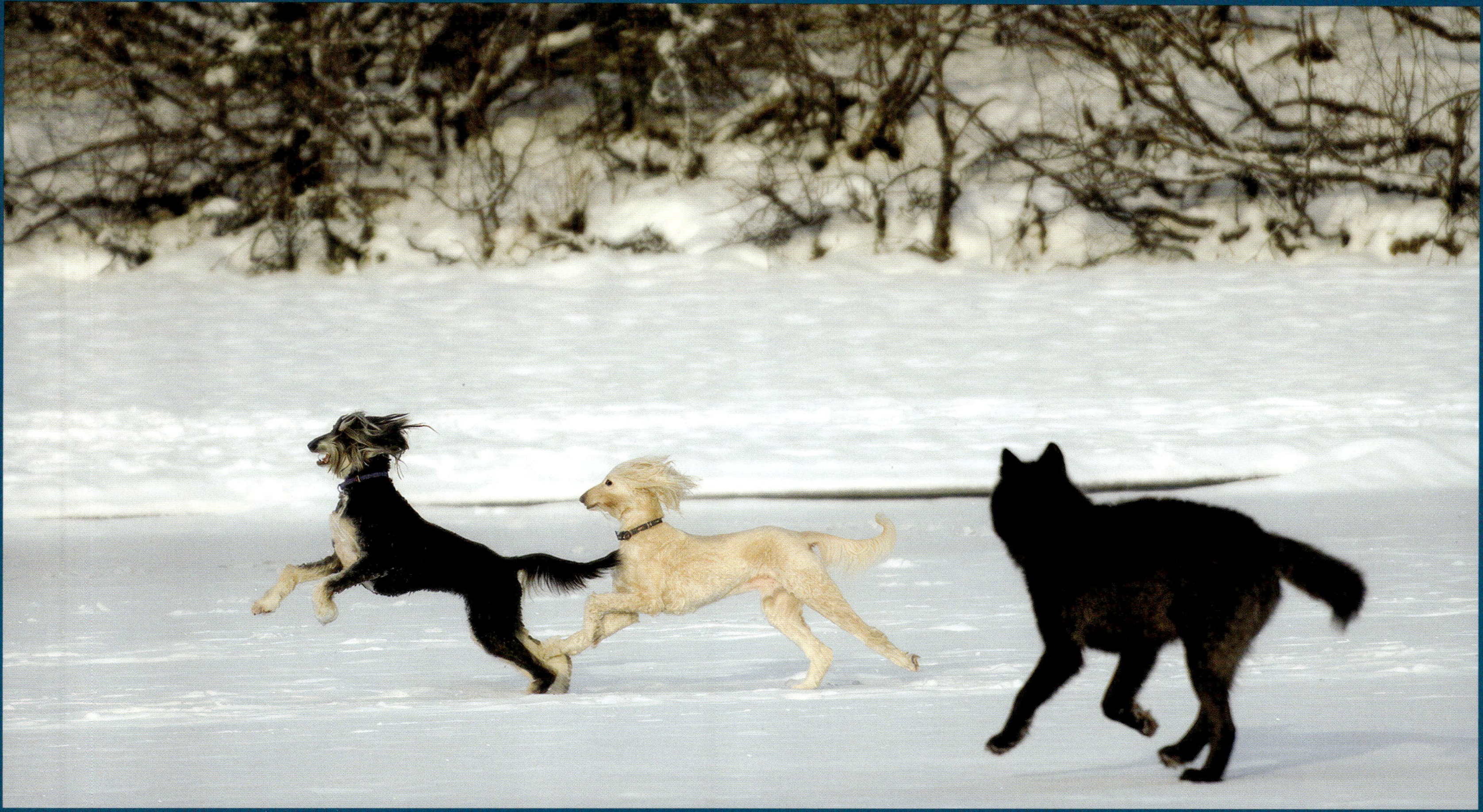

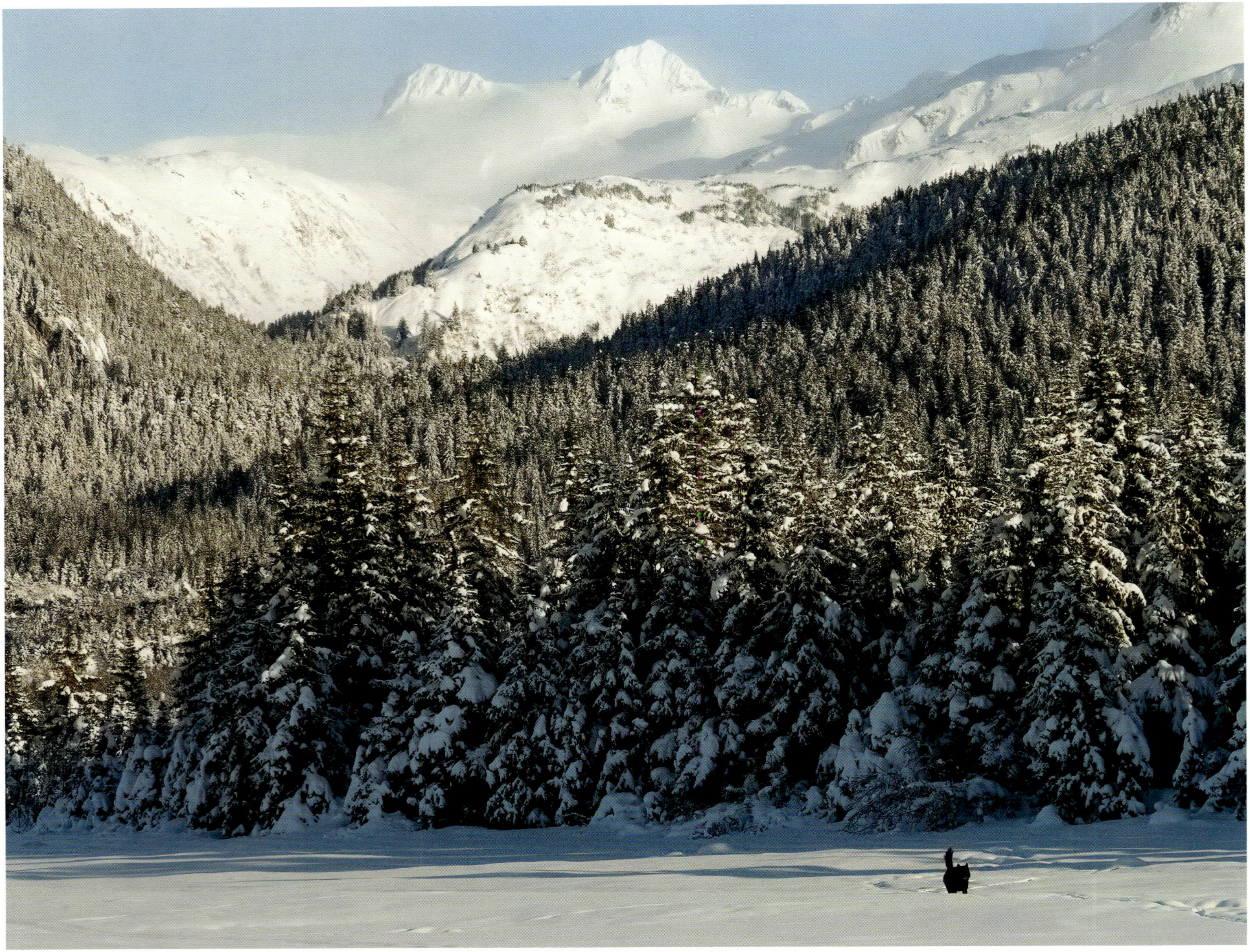

Romeo, as ever—a wolf on the move.

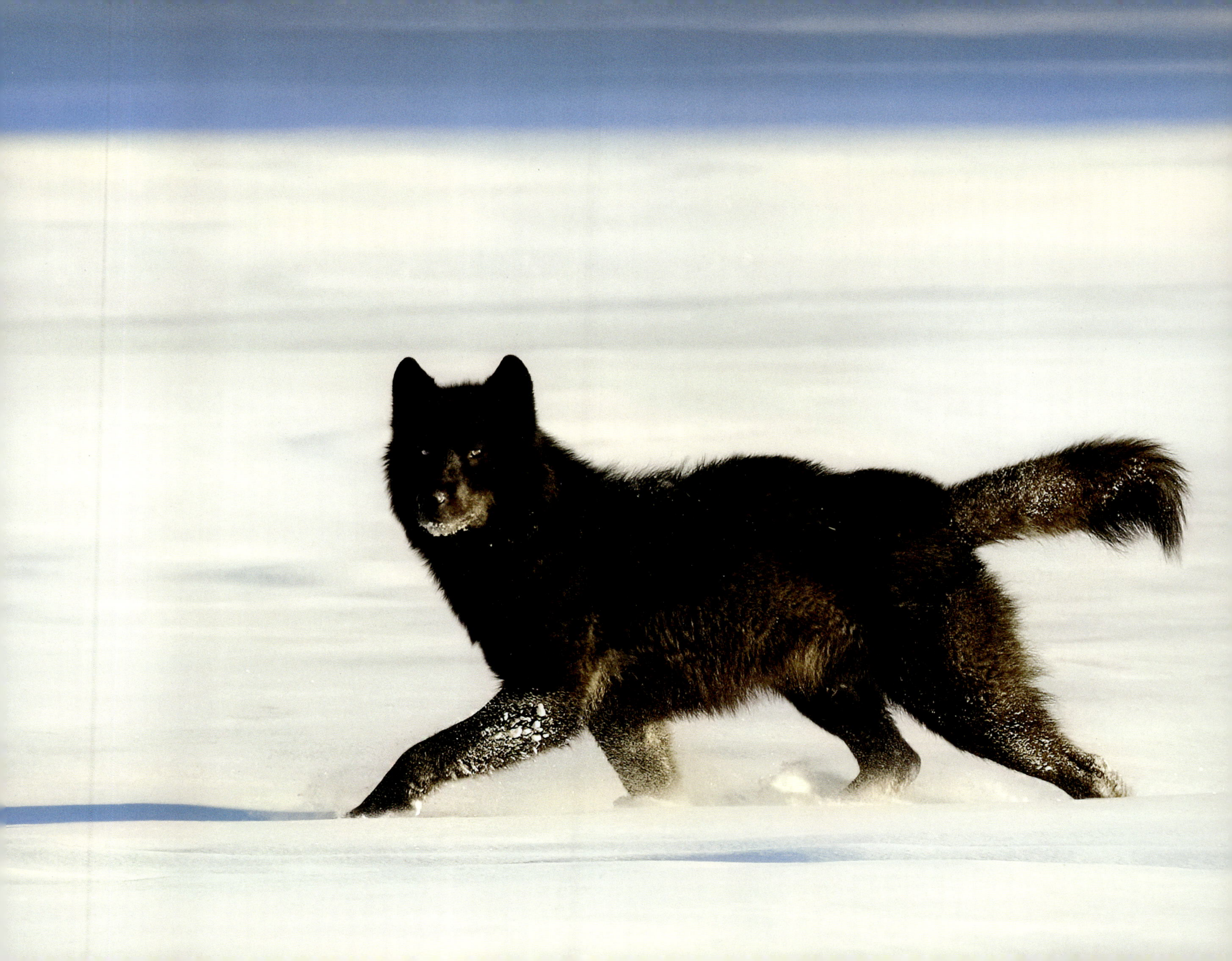

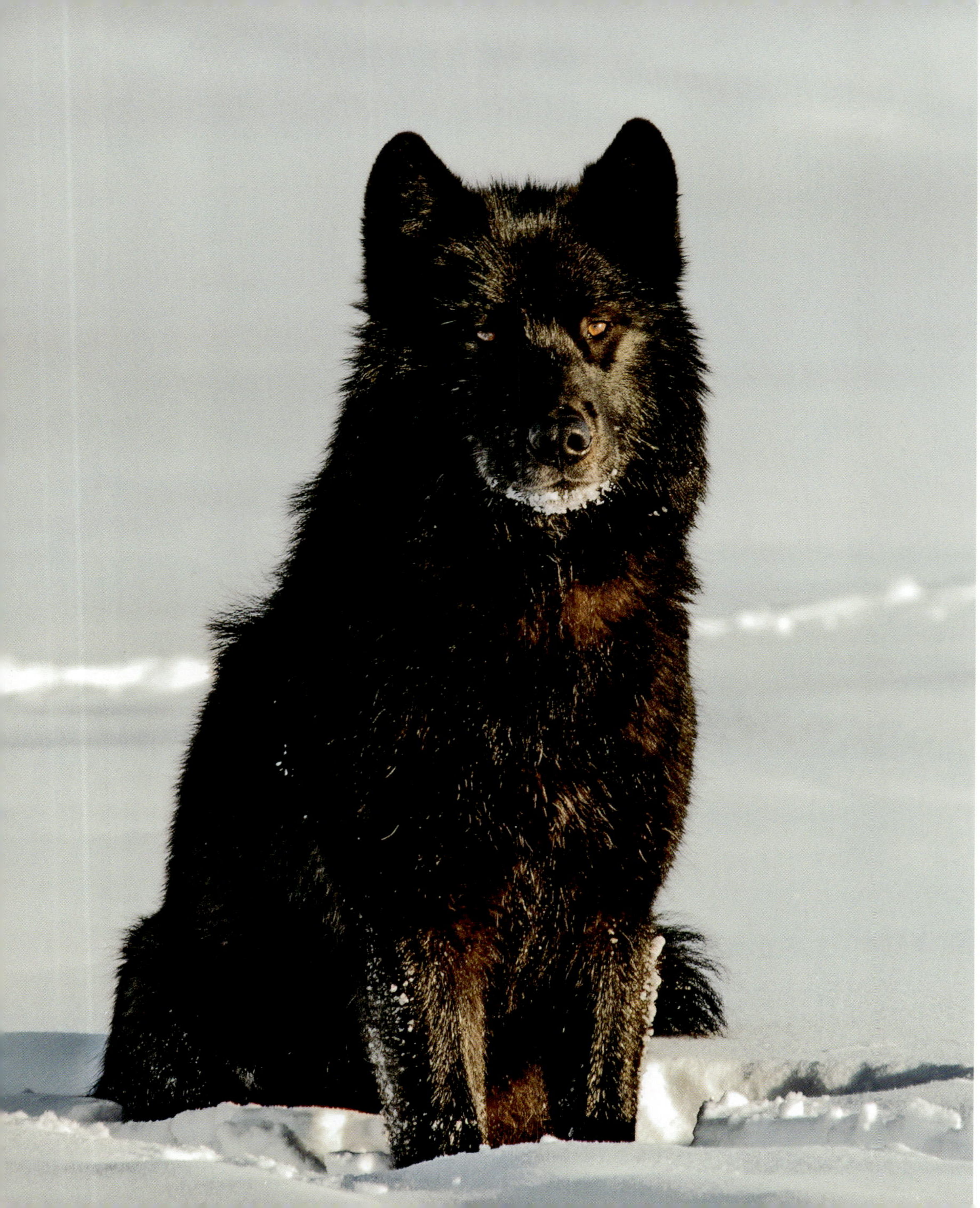

The saga of Juneau's friendly wolf continued over six years.

In those days before Facebook and Instagram's global reach, Romeo remained a local celebrity, holding court out on the lake during the tourist offseason, attended by his adoring home public and paparazzi. Controversy over his presence continued to ebb and flow as we debated what to do or not do with this wolf; and in the process, strengthened our own bonds and sense of community. Oblivious to our wranglings, the wolf came and went, not just surviving, but prospering on his chosen ground. With each spring thaw he faded into the country and returned with autumn's hard frosts; his wanderings, like so many other things about him, shrouded in mystery. But all that we would never know about this wolf we called Romeo were what we loved best.

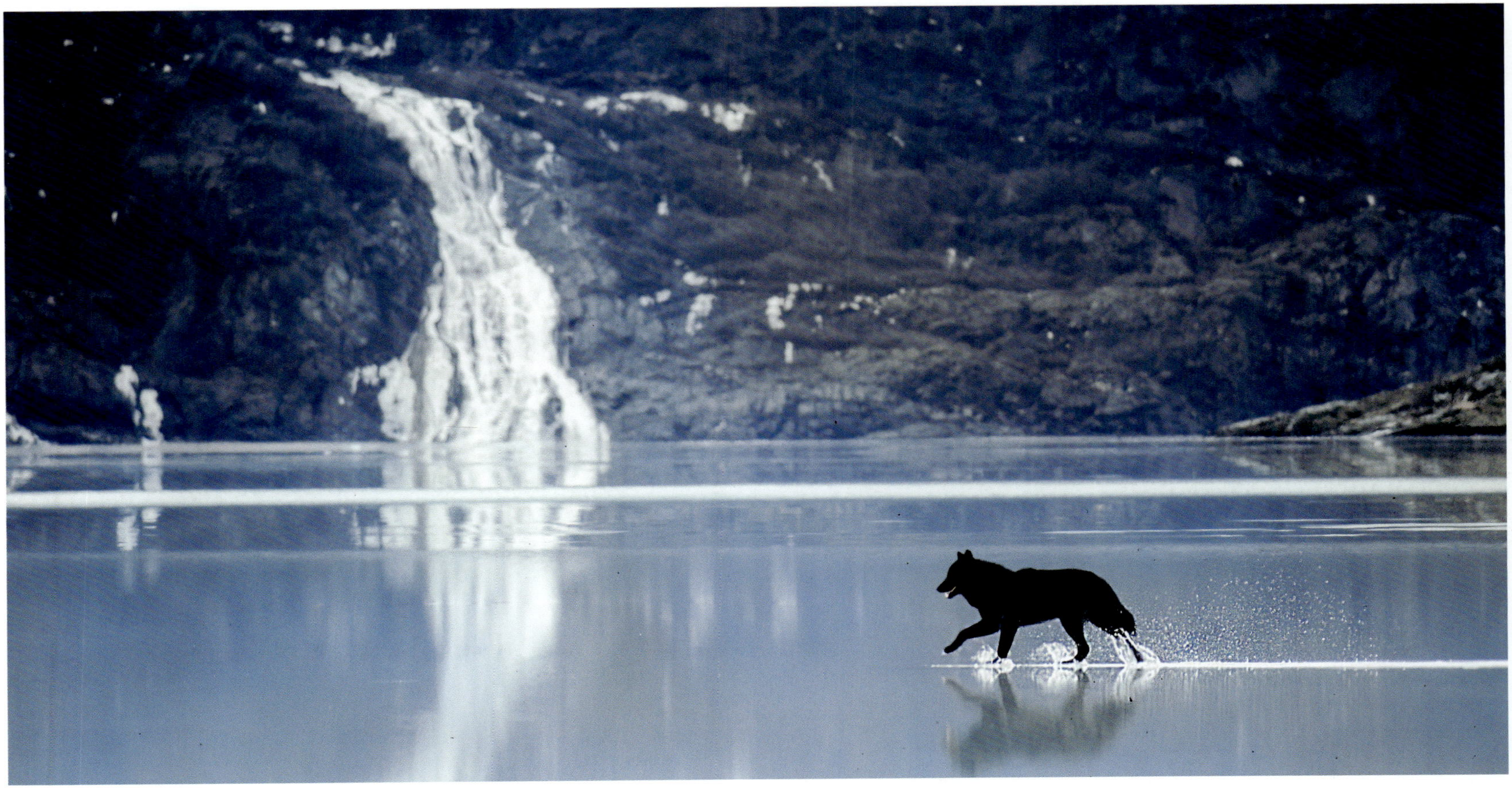

Even during his winter stays he'd sometimes disappear for weeks, and we'd wonder if he'd finally found a mate, or had at last met his end; even without the dangers posed by us, a wolf's life tends toward hard and brief—in Alaska, just two to three years on average.

They starve; suffer disease and accidents; are killed by other wolves in inter-pack strife. In at least his eighth year, perhaps his ninth, Romeo had roughly tripled that life expectancy. Sometimes it seemed he might live forever. But each time I saw him go I watched as if for the last time.

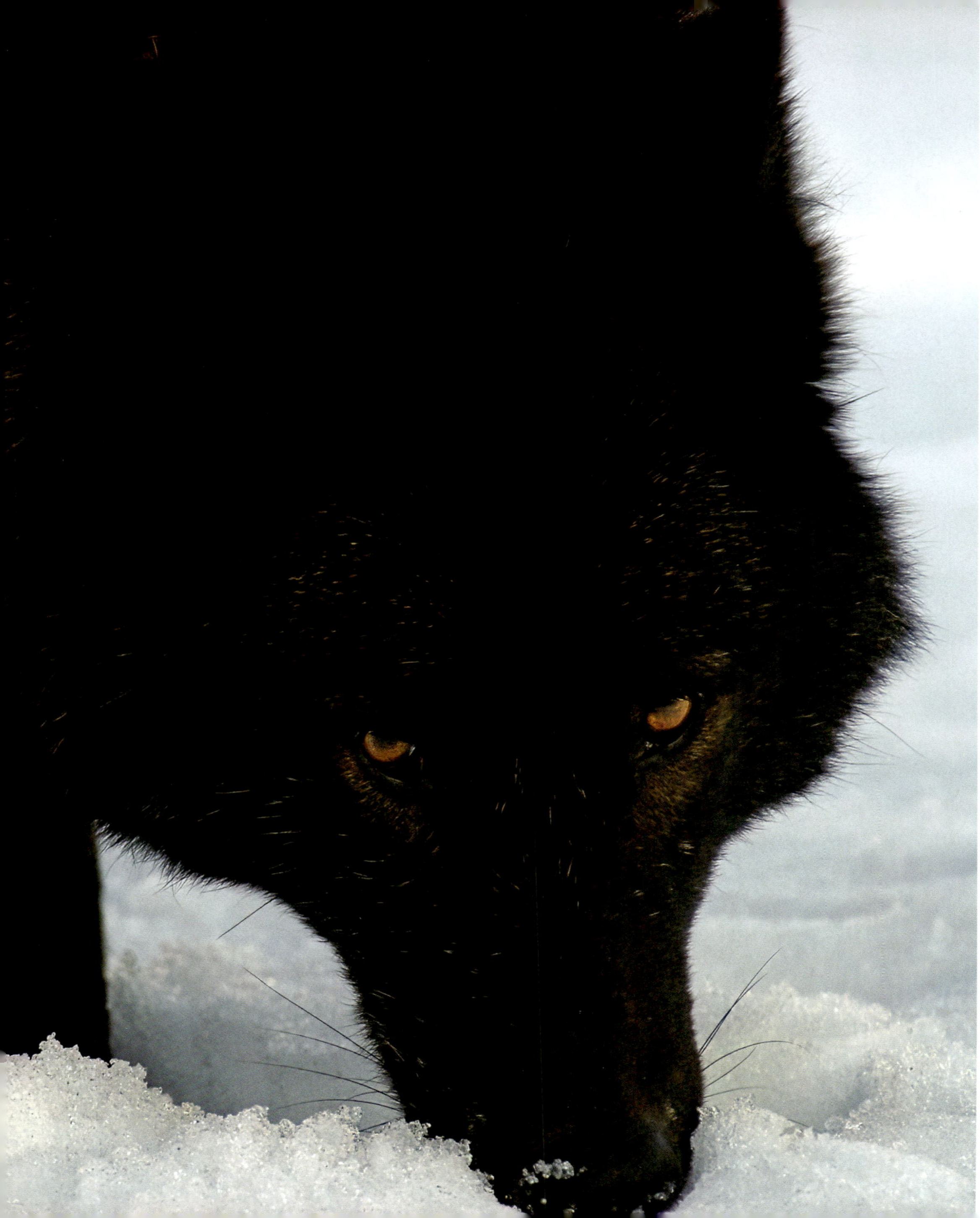

And one day it was. The wolf we called Romeo vanished in early September 2009, there one day to meet Harry then gone, as if he'd never been.

Pretty to imagine him lounging with a mate and pups on a sunny hillside; but he'd been illegally shot by a pair of small-minded poachers and skinned for a trophy. In their boasts—which is how they eventually got caught—the killers flaunted a banal, comic-book evil, openly reveling in the pain they'd caused to so many. A courtroom-packed trial for one of the two culminated in a wrist slap: a lecture by the judge; a couple thousand bucks in fines and a few dozen community service hours never paid nor served. The other killer, out of state, never reached trial. There would be no justice for Romeo in a formal sense; there were no laws or sentencing precedents to suit the crime. The state of Alaska had never placed much value in a wolf, named or not.

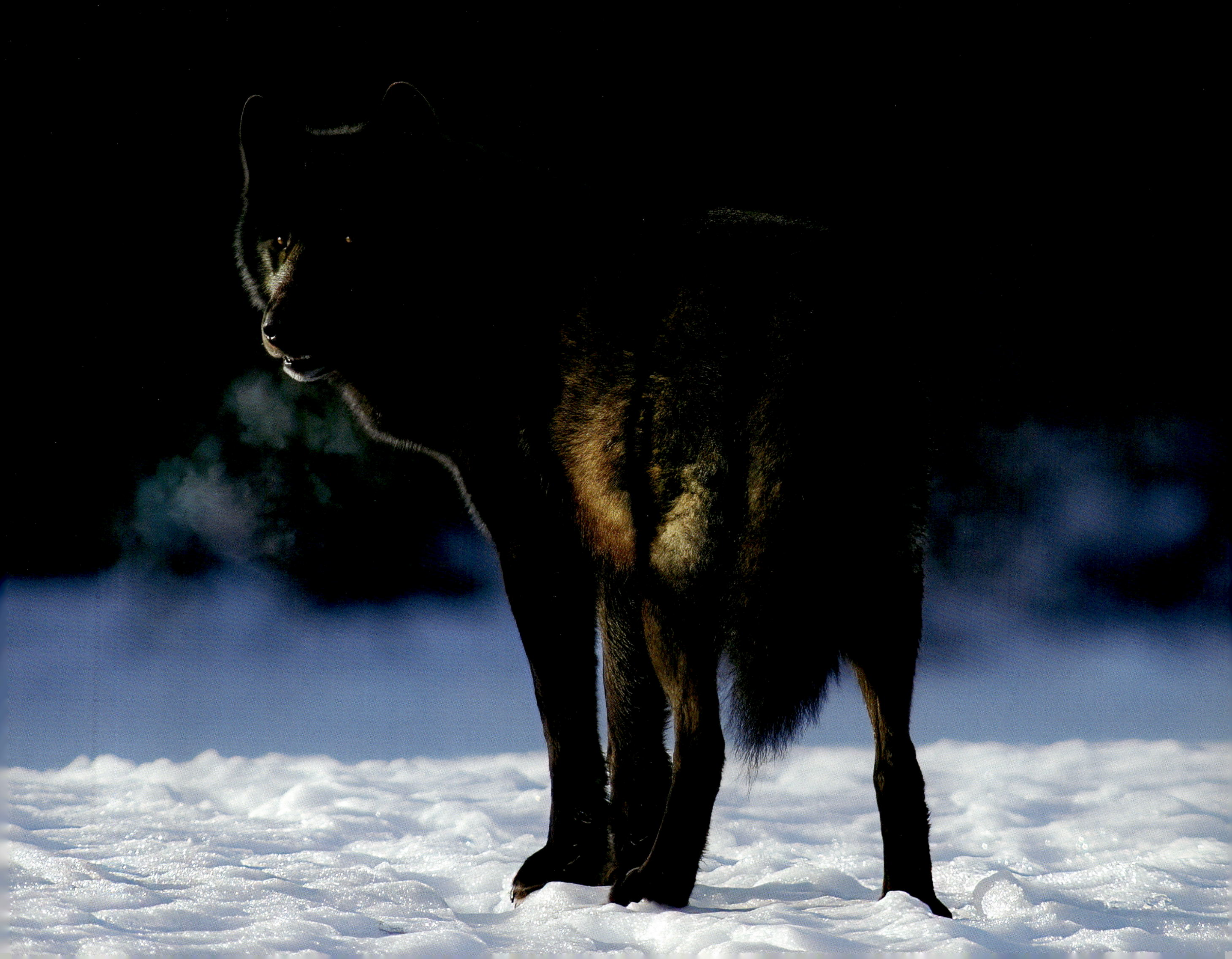

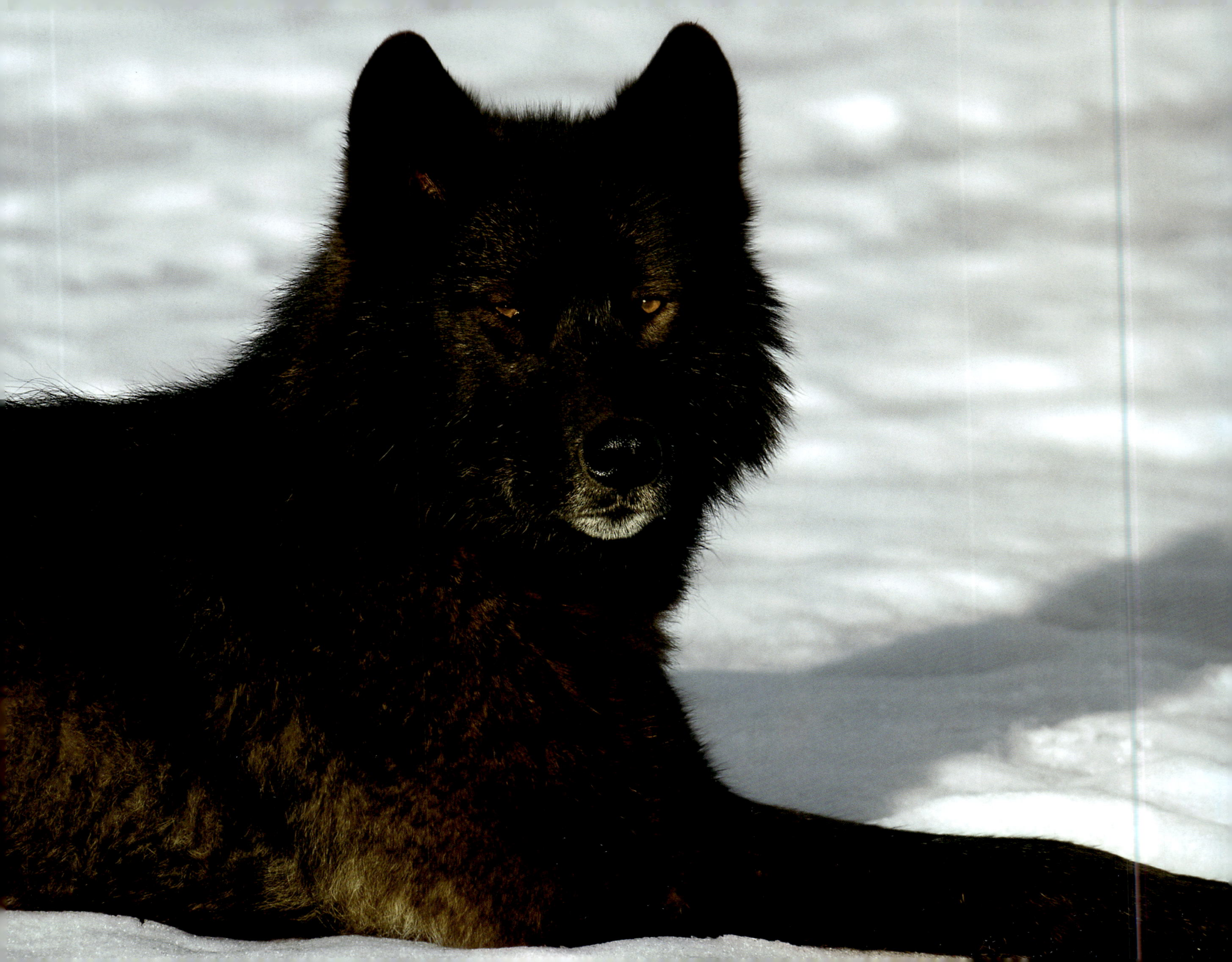

A Romeo Memory

The Last Time

On an early spring afternoon in 2009, Harry Robinson, Brittain, and I hiked the lower West Glacier trail. Romeo joined in, bounding through the snow-deep woods parallel to the trail, sometimes ahead, sometimes behind. At the end of our walk he scaled a berm and seemed to strike a pose. I had no idea we would never meet again.

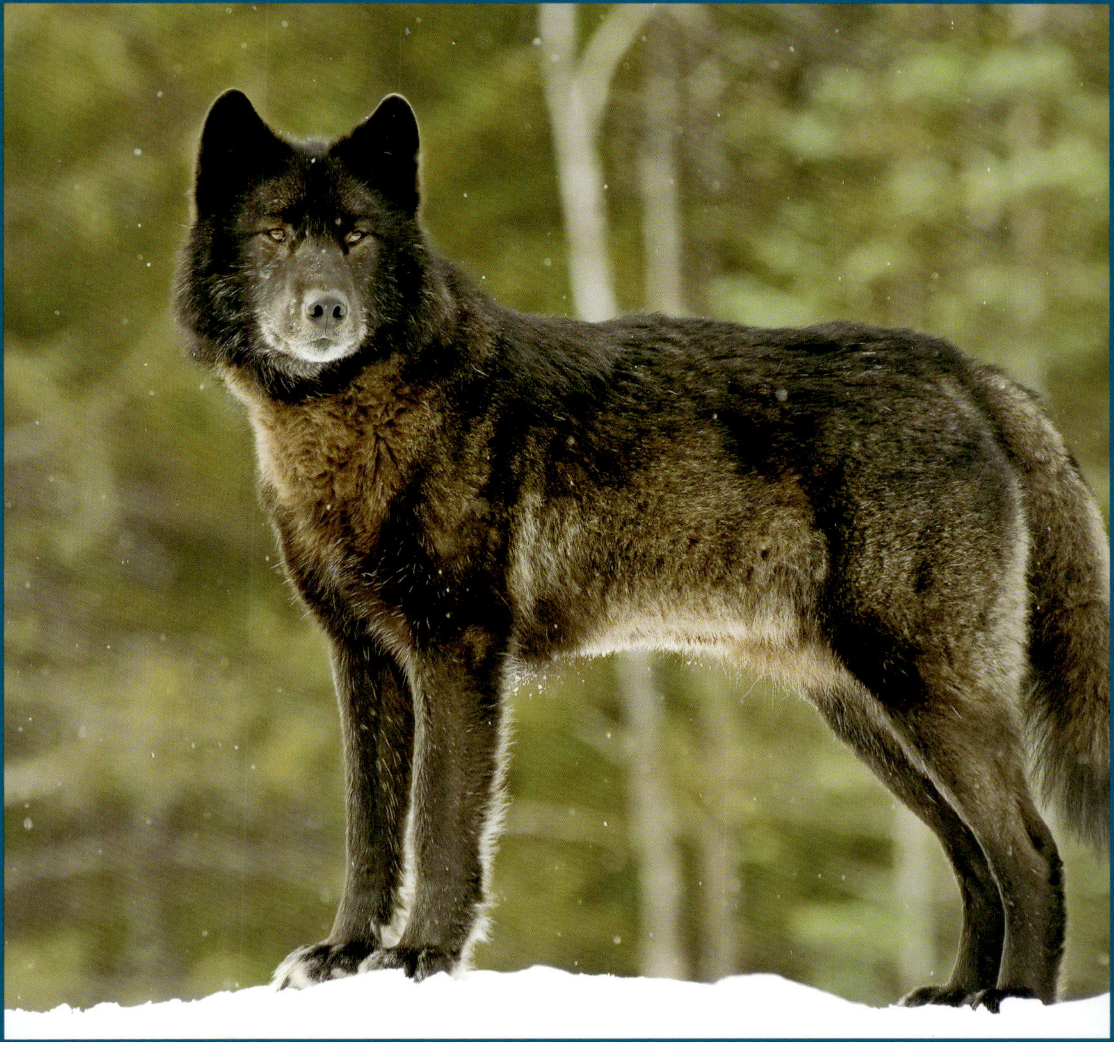

Of course we mourned, together and alone, our grief a hard, deep-raveled trail.

Two weeks after the trial, a year after his death, we held a memorial service on a chill November afternoon out by the Big Rock where Romeo met so many of us—a final-feeling, emotion-laden sendoff—and that could have been that. Memories fade, time passes, and people forget.

Instead, more than a dozen years later, a Romeo exhibit stands inside the Mendenhall Glacier Visitor Center and a bronze plaque near Nugget Falls, both seen by hundreds of thousands of visitors each year. A handful of books, two Juneau streets, a beer or two, and a local brand of coffee have marked the black wolf's time among us, and framed images of him grace homes not just in Juneau but far beyond. Many, too, have told and retold his story, or been prompted into artistic expressions: paintings, computer graphics, photography, music, sculpture. One online slide show, unauthorized but welcome, garnered over 16 million views.

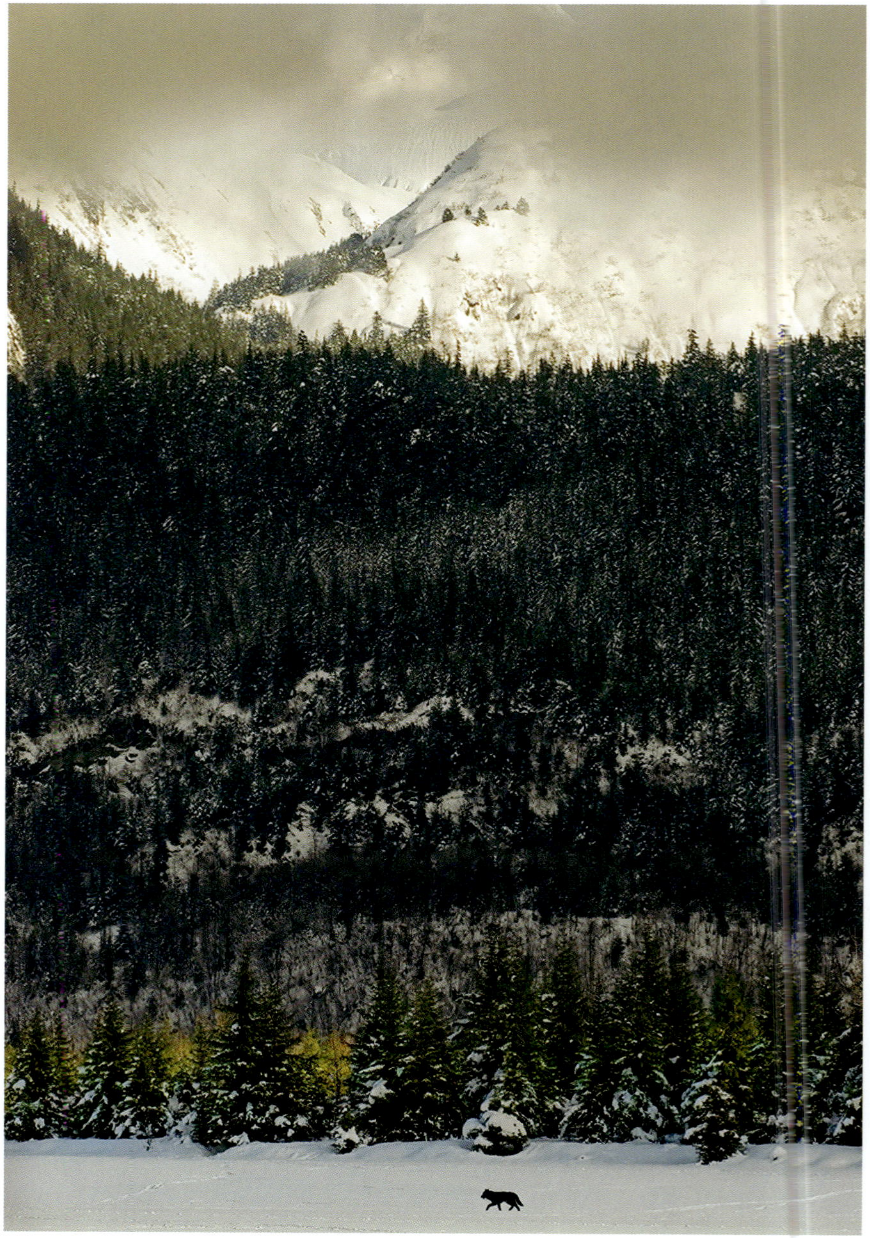

In February 2022, Romeo's spirit returned yet again in a community celebration of his life set in motion by Juneau composer Todd Hunt.

Inspired by Romeo's story and sponsored by the Orpheus Project, a nonprofit arts organization, Todd and fellow composer Emerson Eads created separate works of 'Wolf Music' presented in two-hour live performances integrating symphonic composition, operatic song, image projection, and dance, featuring the Juneau Symphony. A Romeo photo exhibit also was created and displayed at the downtown community arts center, plus a presentation of Romeo's saga, and a cross-country ski event held on the black wolf's home ground by the glacier, where the memory of his howls still echo in the silence.

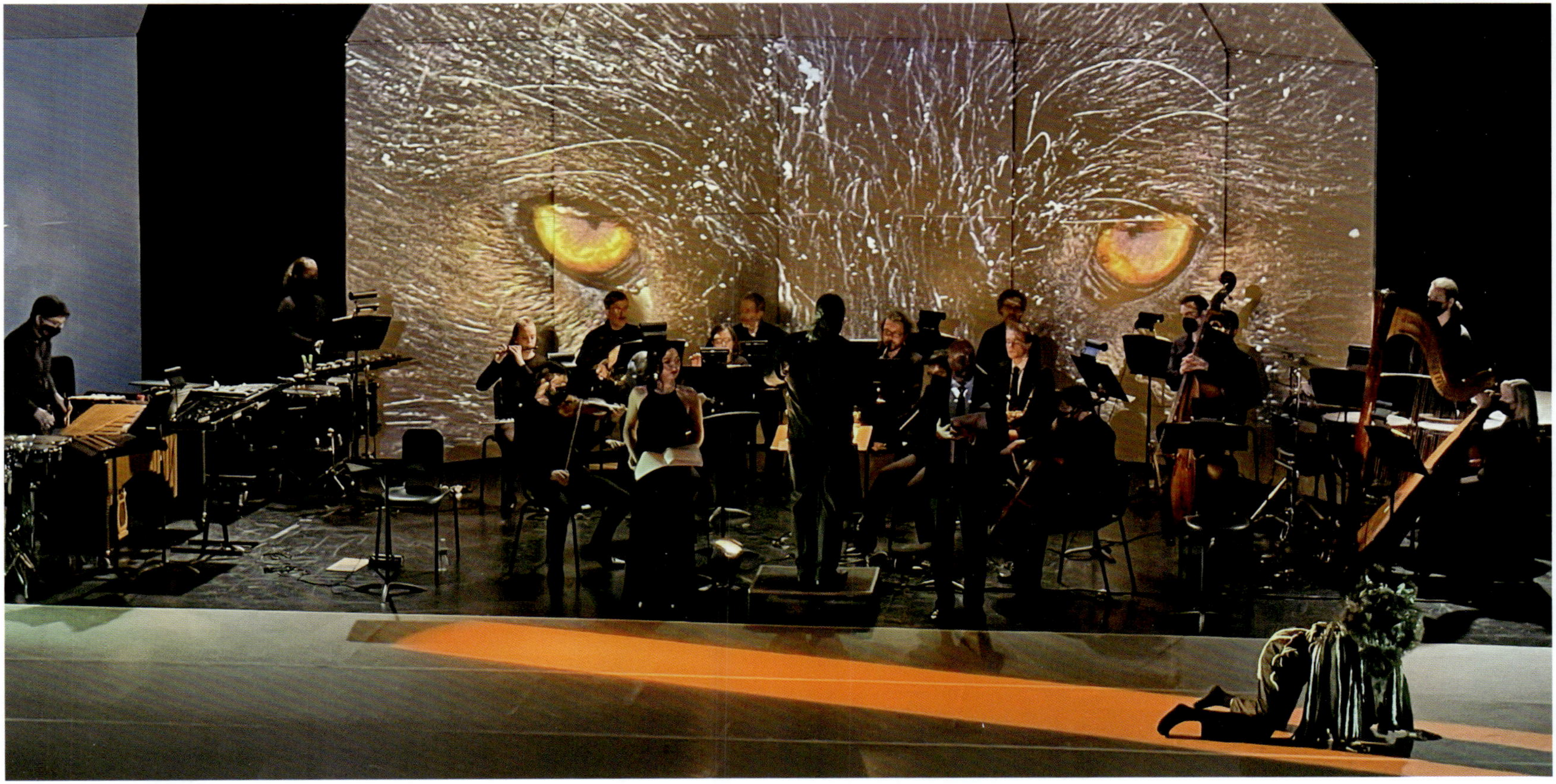

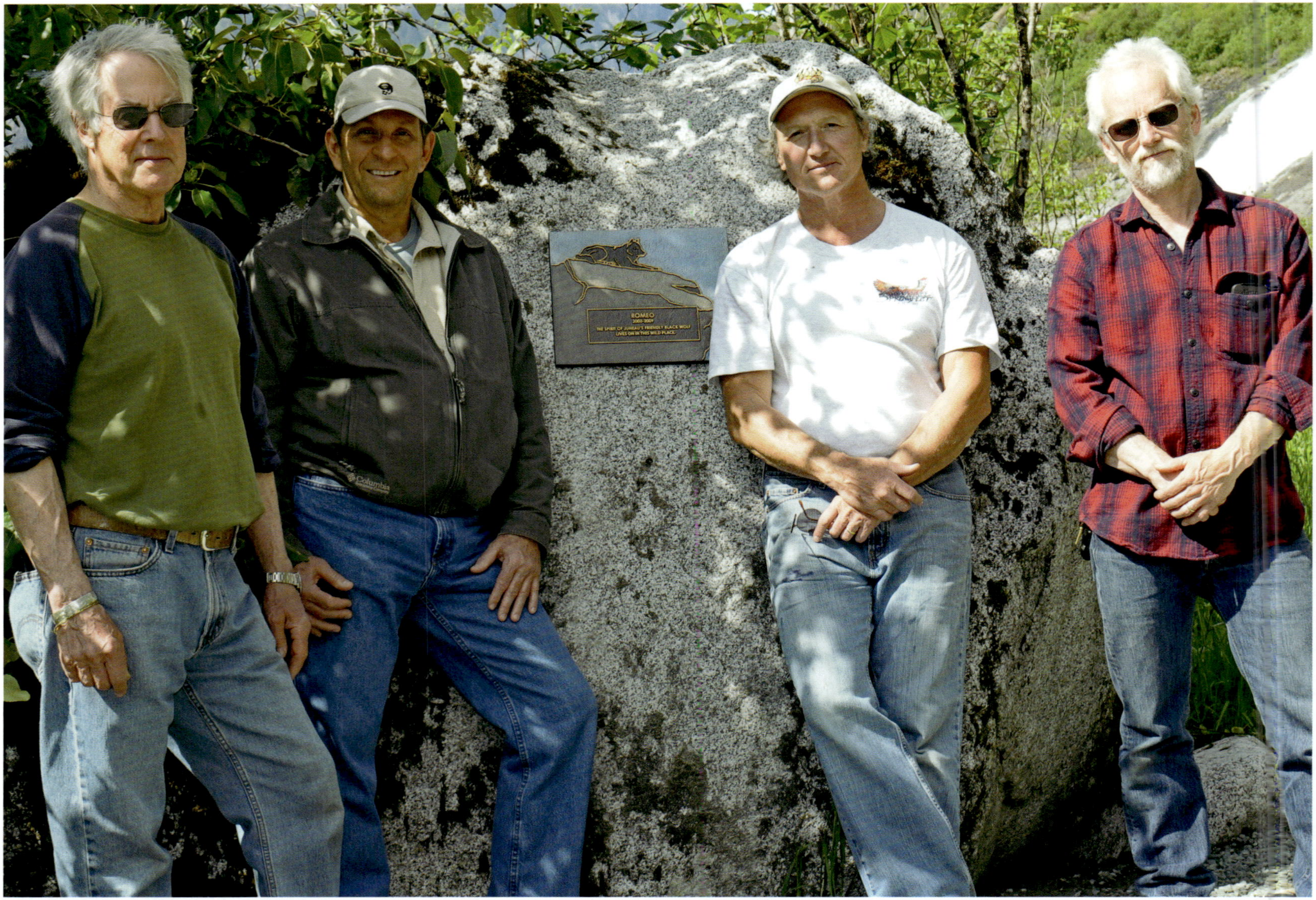

Above: *Joel Bennett, Harry Robinson, Nick Jans and Vic Walker—all friends of Romeo.* **Right**: *Evie Walker at Romeo's 2022 exhibit*

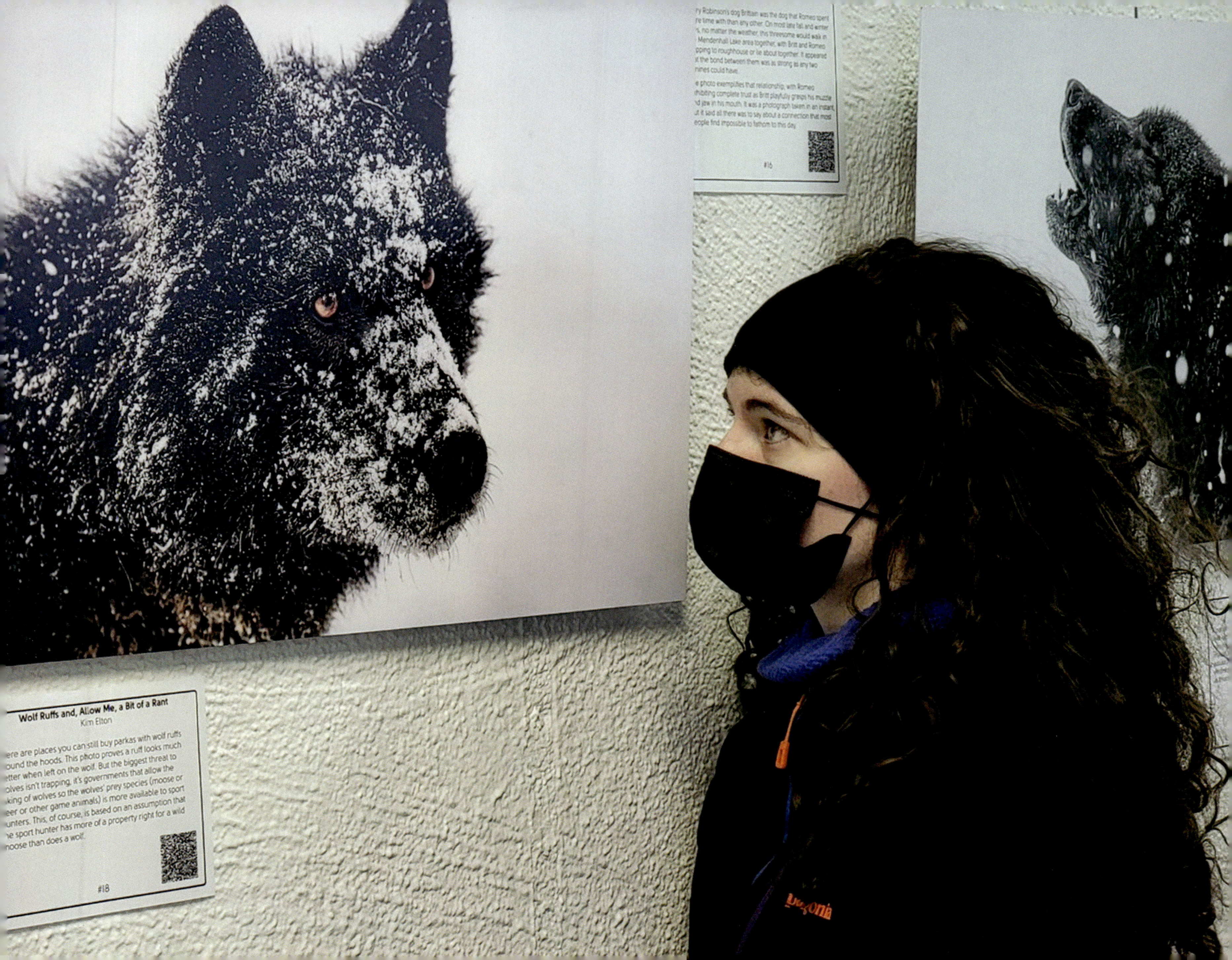

Wolf Ruffs and, Allow Me, a Bit of a Rant
Kim Elton
ere are places you can still buy parkas with wolf ruffs ound the hoods. This photo proves a ruff looks much etter when left on the wolf. But the biggest threat to olves isn't trapping, it's governments that allow the king of wolves so the wolves' prey species (moose or eer or other game animals) is more available to sport unters. This, of course, is based on an assumption that he sport hunter has more of a property right for a wild noose than does a wolf.
#18
ry Robinson's dog Brittain was the dog that Romeo spent re time with than any other. On most late fall and winter s, no matter the weather, this threesome would walk in Mendenhall Lake area together, with Britt and Romeo pping to roughhouse or lie about together. It appeared at the bond between them was as strong as any two nines could have.
e photo exemplifies that relationship, with Romeo hibiting complete trust as Britt playfully grasps his muzzle d jaw in his mouth. It was a photograph taken in an instant, ut it said all there was to say about a connection that most eople find impossible to fathom to this day.
#16
patagonia

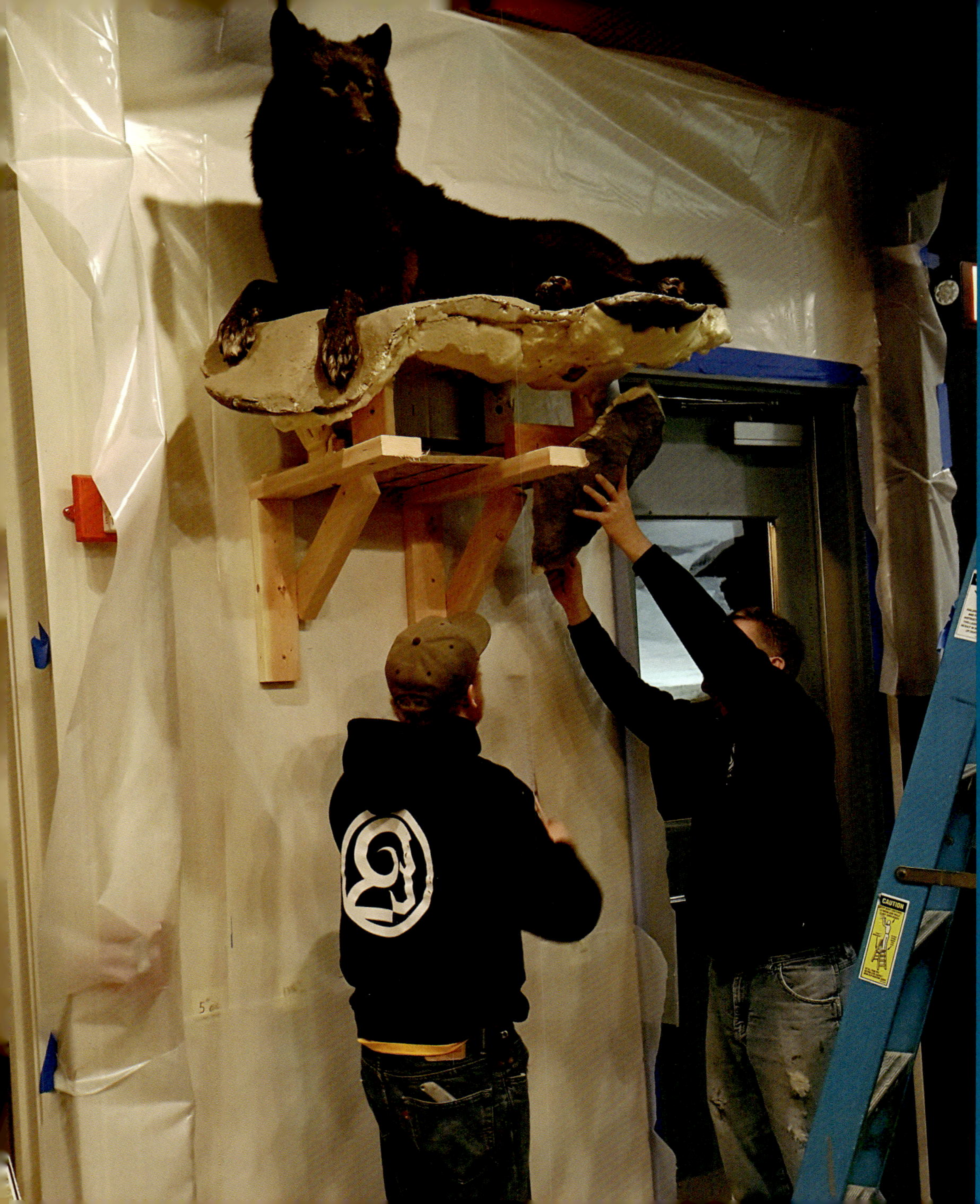

Building a Memory

Though Romeo died in 2009, the exhibit honoring him at the Mendenhall Glacier Visitor Center was slow in coming. Waiting for the legal process to play out, obtaining Romeo's court-confiscated skin, wangling the necessary permission, raising tens of thousands of dollars, and coordinating the right specialized craftsmen/artists took seven years. But once started, the actual construction took just four days. Romeo's name and story being absent from the exhibit stands as testament to the nature of Alaska wolf politics in general, and those surrounding Juneau's friendly wolf in particular. But there Romeo curls in a relaxed, familiar pose, watching for dogs. Hundreds of Juneauites attended the dedication ceremony on a blustery winter night

The builders at work.

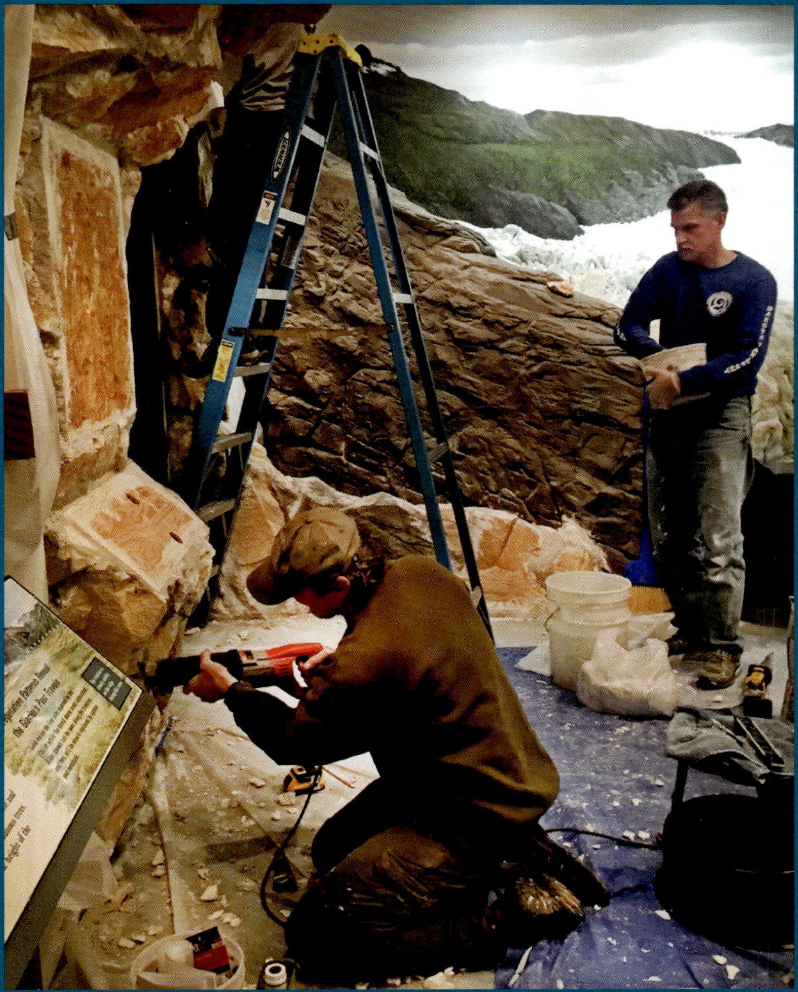

Nick with a power saw, hands on, start to finish.

Romeo gazes out over his home ground.

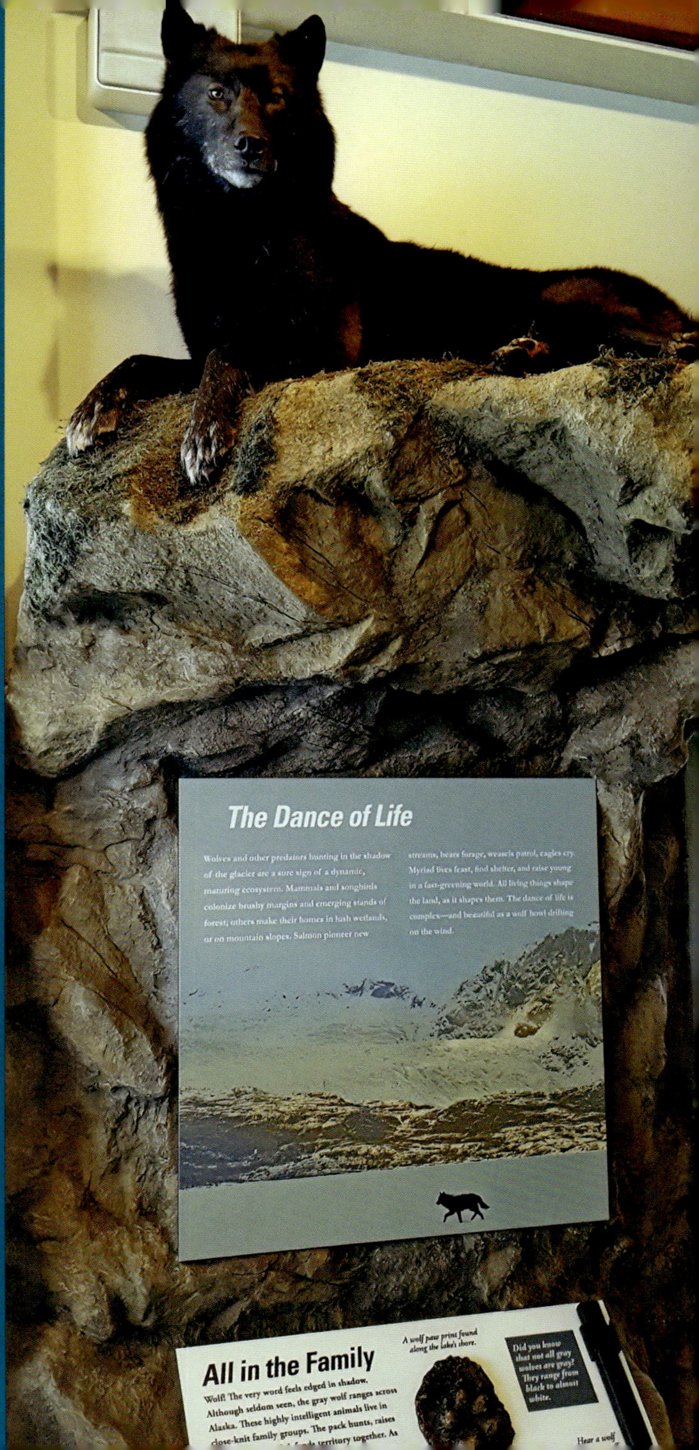

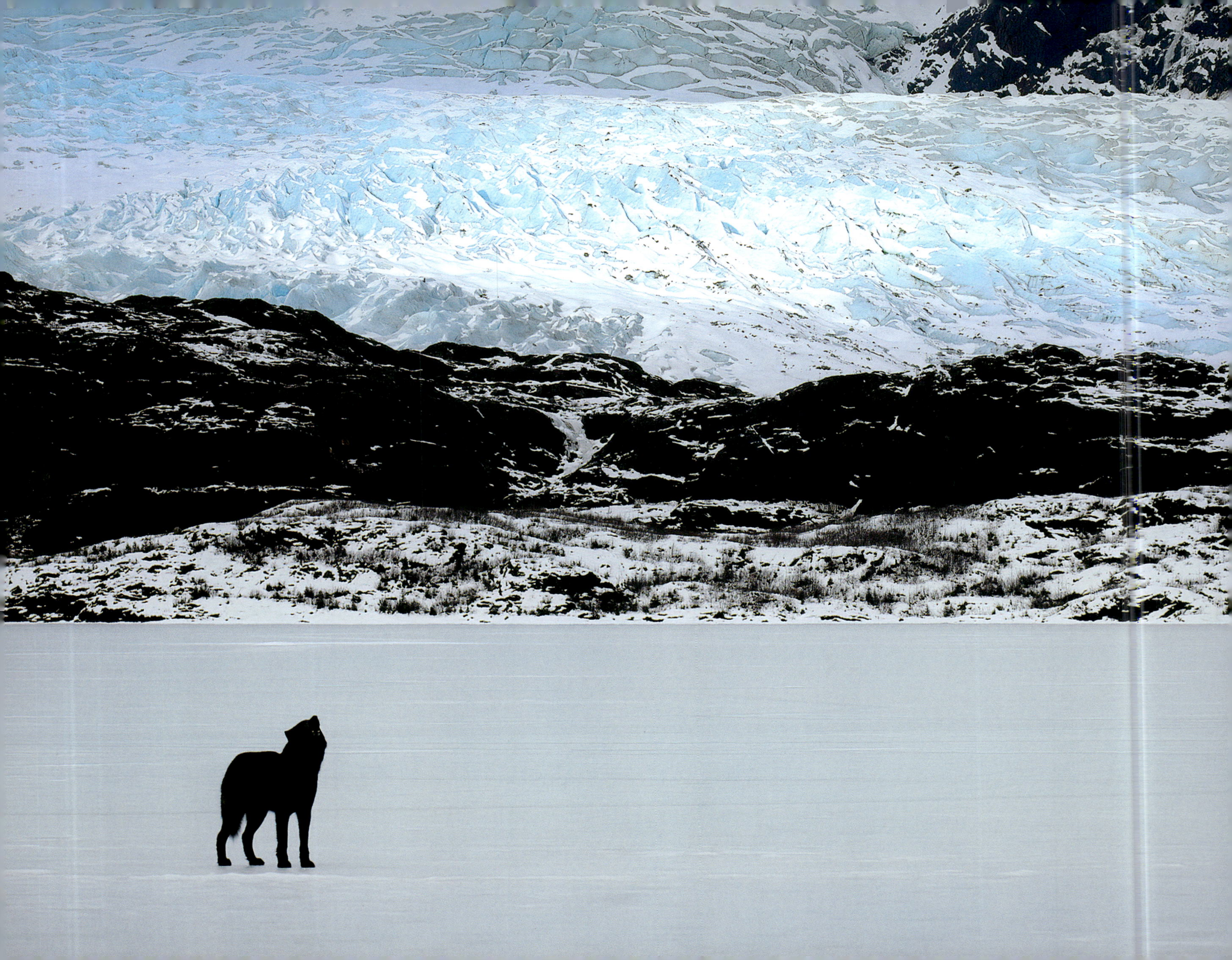

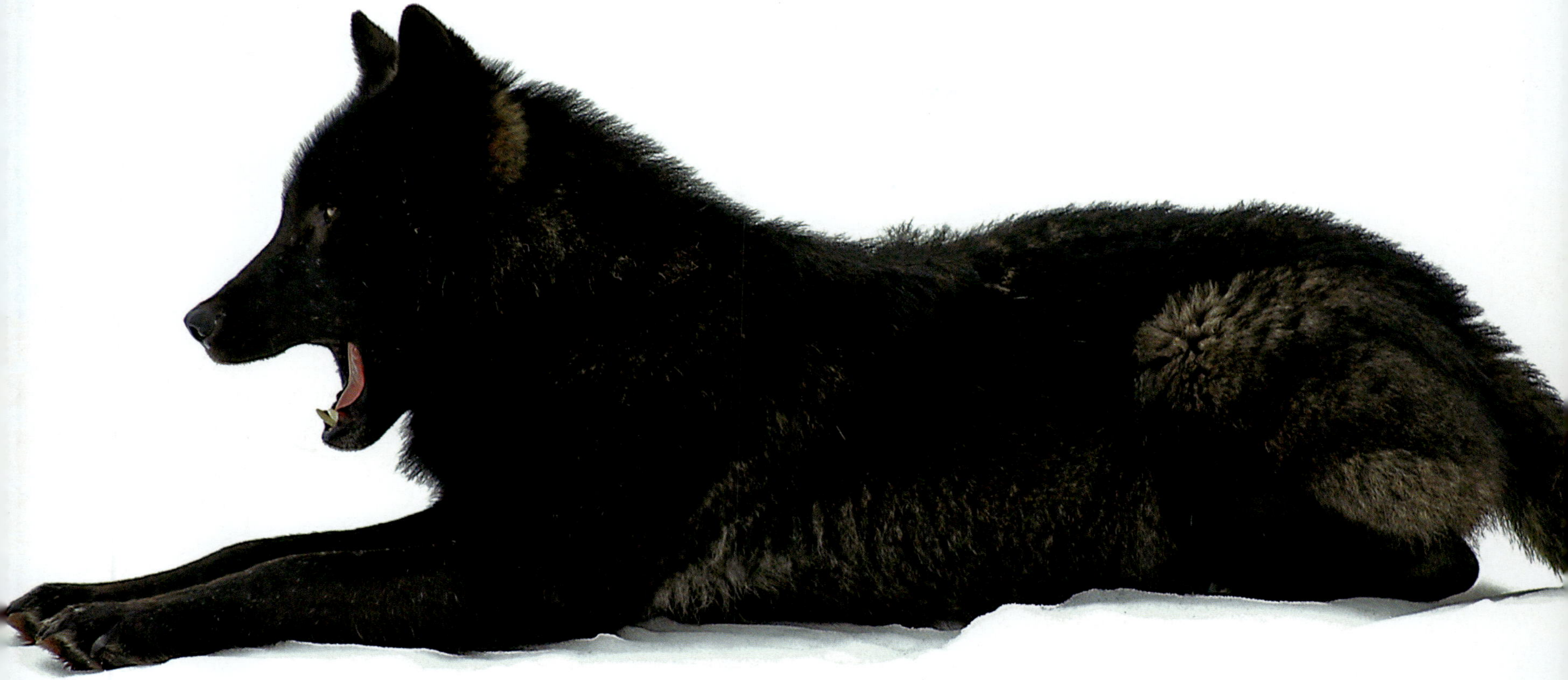

So it was that a lone black wolf came to live among us, became woven into Juneau's story, part of who we are. We knew him as neighbor and friend, as he knew us. But this is what matters: Years from now, parents will tell their kids, Once upon a time, there was a wolf called Romeo. And they'll remember.

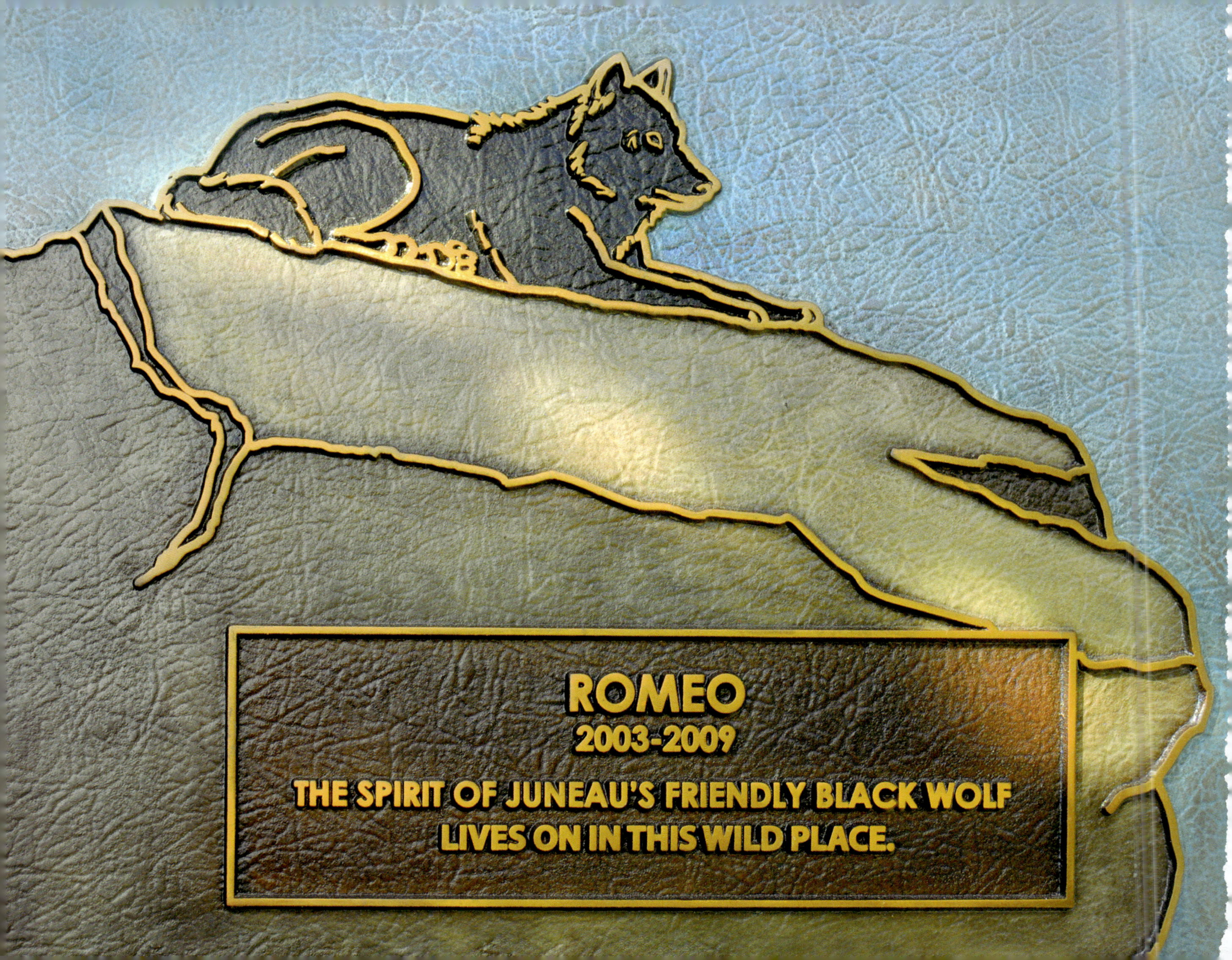
ROMEO
2003-2009
THE SPIRIT OF JUNEAU'S FRIENDLY BLACK WOLF
LIVES ON IN THIS WILD PLACE.